D1487337

Communicating Christ In a Religious World

by

John Thomas Rogers

Revised Edition
December 2009
Original Title: Communicating Christ to the Cults

xulon
PRESS

Dedication to Original Edition

This book is not dedicated to the scholar who knows his Bible backward and forward theologically and is therefore ready to tackle any error, but rather to the inexperienced Christian who does not know what to say, but very desperately wants to share Christ with those who believe in "another Jesus."

Dedication to Revised Edition

To Jeremiah, who, despite challenges that would leave most of us in despair, continues to pursue his goal of communicating Christ to those around him.

Contents

What Causes Cults? * Definition of a Cult * Cults
Are Effective * Cults Are Evolving * Purpose of This
Book

Witnessing with an Attitude * Nature of Religion *
Cults and Conflicts * Right Tools * Love of God *
Knowledge of the Bible

Opening Comments * Discussion Principles *
Establish Authority * Bible Cult * Book of Mormon

Baptism for the Dead * Eternal Marriages * Lost Tribes of Israel * One Hundred and Forty-four Thousand * Preexistence * Reincarnation * Soul Sleep: Eternity versus Annihilation

Temporary Alternative to Discussion * Proper Use of Anti-Cult Material * Suggested Visitation Passages * Bible As Far As Translated Correctly * Point of No Discussion * Ephesians 2:8-9 and the Mormons * John 1:1 and the Jehovah's Witnesses * Prophecy and the Cults

False Authority * False Gospel * False Jesus * Urgency of the Gospel

Foreword to
Original Edition

Normally, in a teacher-student relationship, the teacher by definition teaches, and the student learns. But with John Rogers, I found the situation to be reversed many times. In this particular situation, the instructor learned as much as the student. I found John to be a bottomless resource of information about Mormonism. He probably has a better grasp of Mormonism and its teaching than do ninety-five percent of all Latter-day Saints.

Despite his young age, John is well qualified by study and thousands of hours of witnessing to Mormons and other cultists to write this book.

I highly recommend this book - not just to be read, but to also be applied. Read it! Study it! Absorb it! Then wait until the Lord leads two young, smartly dressed, bike-riding men to knock on your door, and put its contents to use.

Martin R. Dahlquist
Academic Dean
Spurgeon Baptist Bible College
Mulberry, Florida
1983

Acknowledgments

I could not possibly give credit to all of the many people who helped prepare me for the writing of this book. A few deserve special mention: my mom and dad, who first started me seriously studying the Bible when I was seven, and Dr. Martin Dahlquist, my college theology teacher, a man who has a talent for putting the difficult into understandable language. I also must specially thank Lloyd and Martha Larkin, the missionaries in Utah under whom I worked as an apprentice missionary (without whom I might never have sensed my burden for the Mormons). Lloyd's ministry and his patient instruction of my developing understanding of religious people taught me many of the core concepts of witnessing to cult individuals. Whatever is right about this book, he most certainly influenced. For whatever is wrong about my conclusions, I bear sole responsibility. Lloyd, I will forever be in your debt!

One individual I cannot forget to mention is Beabea, who as a loving young missionary wife stood by me and encouraged me as I wrote the original book during the challenging period of pre-field ministry. I want to also thank my daughter, Christy, for her many hours of typing the book back into the computer for the revised edition, and my son, Jeremiah, for his research into the 1 Peter passages to be used in this new edition.

I also need to recognize three important ladies. Although the revised edition of this book was redone on a computer, as almost everything else is today, the original edition was done in the old-fashioned way with typewriter and correction fluid. Therefore, I once again want to thank Mrs. Edwin Chapin for proof-reading the original manuscript of the first edition and offering her excellent suggestions. I also wish to thank Mrs. Helen Lampe for typing the final version of the original manuscript. Finally, I want to thank Mrs. Anna Unroe, who with her husband, Elzie, has served many years as a missionary among the Native American Sioux and ultimately in ministry in Utah to Mormons. She also had the distinction of being my secretary at Evangelical Baptist Missions for several years. With no thought of personal benefit (although I did promise to take her and her hubby out to dinner), Anna reviewed the manuscript and offered her usual excellent suggestions.

Another individual that I want to very much thank for his recent efforts is Chris Vlachos, who did the research for the John 1:1 section of the revised edition. Most of what is contained in that section is the work of his brilliant mind. I would also like to thank Sharilyn Grayson for her final edit of the book before publishing. Most books owe their quality to a good editor, and I am fortunate to have had one.

Finally, ultimately, always, I wish to thank the Lord Jesus Christ, the One who gives purpose and meaning to this book.

Introduction

Coming of the Cults

Y ou are sitting in your living room reading a book. You hear a knock at your door. As you rise to answer it, you notice through the window two bicycles parked in the driveway. Opening the door, you discover two clean-cut young men dressed in white shirts, ties, dress slacks, and possibly suit coats. They appear to be conservative salesman or Christian seminary students. However, they inform you that they are members of the Church of Jesus Christ of Latter-day Saints, the Mormons. Your mind races. What do you say?

You respond, "We are Christians; we believe in Jesus Christ."

They reply, "So do we. We are Christians who believe in the Christ also."

Confused, you catch yourself saying, "But I thought you guys were a cult..."

Assignment: Using only your Bible, answer the following questions or propositions:

1. How do I know the Bible is complete?
2. How do I know God's truth has not been lost?
3. Prove Jesus is God.
4. Prove there is only one God.
5. Prove Jesus is not the brother of Satan.
6. Prove humans did not live in a spiritual preexistence before coming to earth, being either good or bad spirit children.
7. Prove that God the Father does not have a physical body.
8. Explain why you do not baptize for dead people.

Most people initially think that some of these points are so ridiculous that even bothering with them is pointless. Some people today in the United States, however, believe these concepts and take them very seriously. These uniquely different ideas are part of Mormon (the Church of Jesus Christ of Latter-day Saints) doctrine. Mormons believe that the Bible is incomplete; that the truth of God has been lost and restored through them; that Jesus is deity but not the same God as God the Father; that more gods exist than just the ruling God of our earth; that Jesus is the brother of Satan; that we did live in a preexistence; that God has a body; and finally, that baptizing for the dead is necessary.

The Mormons are not the only group with unusual doctrines. Beginning in the 1800s, a new type of religion began appearing in Christendom. Unlike the different groups already in existence that claimed to be orthodox and right, these new groups took a step in a different direction. Most of the discussion in church history had centered on the doctrines of the Bible as the only Word of God and salvation as a product of works or grace or both. The new groups attacked an area that had rarely been touched since the early days of the church age (although they also maintained the controversy over salvation and the Bible). This new area of attack was against the persons of God and Jesus Christ.

The attack was not direct but very subtle, for it came from people who claimed, on the surface, to believe in Jesus Christ and God. Many of them were very sincere. In 1820, Joseph Smith and Mormonism appeared on the scene. In 1875, Mary Baker Eddy planted seeds that grew into the Christian Science movement. Also, we dare not forget Charles Taze Russell, who in 1879 started his Zion's Watchtower and Herald of Christ's Presence. This group became the Jehovah's Witnesses. The 1900s saw the rise of many more groups that questioned the persons of God and Jesus Christ. Today, modern false prophets are abundant. Apparently, the United States now has over two thousand religions and cults.

The Bible foretold that this proliferation of cults would happen: "Then if any man shall say unto you, Lo, here is Christ, or there; believe it not. For there shall arise false Christs, and false prophets, and shall shew great signs and wonders; insomuch that, if it were possible, they shall deceive the very elect" (Matthew 24:23-24). "Now the Spirit speaketh expressly, that in the latter times some shall depart from the faith, giving heed to seducing spirits, and doctrines of devils" (1 Timothy 4:1).

What Causes Cults?

Where do cults come from? How do they begin? The answers to these questions are as varied as the cults themselves. Many cults, however, do have one central thread in common: misunderstanding scripture. Mormonism is a good example. This cult builds its foundation on a Bible verse! James 1:5 states: "If any of you lack wisdom, let him ask of God, that giveth to all men liberally, and upbraideth not; and it shall be given him." Joseph Smith, the founder of the Mormon Church, believed that this verse was a personal revelation to him instructing him to seek divine revelation to his question, "What is the true church?" In a hidden grove of trees near Palmyra, New York, young Joseph prayed and, according to him, received a vision that no church was true and that he was selected by God to start the true one.

I remember as a child reading John 1:6, "There was a man sent from God, whose name was John." The lights came on in my head as I analyzed the verse. My name was John! I ran into the kitchen shouting to my mother, "Mom! Mom! I'm sent from God!"

She responded calmly, "Oh, really? How do you know that?"

I told her about the Bible verse, John 1:6, and then said, "My name is John, and the verse says there was a man named John sent from God. Therefore, I must be sent from God!"

My mother wisely informed me, "Son, that's how cults get started!"

I have never forgotten the truth she taught me that day, even though it was devastating at the time. Why was I wrong? Why was Joseph Smith wrong? The answer is that a verse of the Bible may have many applications, but only one interpretation. What is the difference? Interpretation should rely on facts, like what the writing of the verse is precisely about, who is actually talking or being talked about, what is literally being talked about, who is actually listening, what exact set of circumstances are occurring, and what is actually happening to the historic people involved. An application is a possible principle or truth I learn from the proper interpretation of the verse. An application must never be taken as divine revelation from God, because it simply could be wrong.

The interpretation of John 1:6 was that God had sent John the Baptist on a mission. A possible application that could be derived from the verse is that God calls people to various tasks, and God might one day send me on a mission for Him. The interpretation of James 1:5 is that God will help the person to be wise who asks Him for wisdom. This interpretation is not divine revelation, just simply being wise. The application is that I have the right as a child of God to ask God to help me be wise in my decision-making. It does not mean that He has to give me a vision. If God meant a vision, then, based on this verse, everyone who asks should have a vision, for the verse tells us that God will do the same for all.

Definition of a Cult

Webster's dictionary defines a cult as a group or organization adhering to or following one individual or his doctrine. [1] This definition would distinguish a cult from the traditional view of a religion that has many varied doctrines and a multitude of leadership. In actuality, Webster's definition applies more to the formation of a group. Normally, cults are misunderstood and rejected. They tend to be isolated from the normal religious realm and to go through a process of time before being accepted. A simple definition of a cult might be that a cult is a religion that has not yet achieved respectability or has not grown up yet – a baby religion! Some cults are never accepted; they never grow up to achieve respectability in the religious world.

Even though all cults are evolving religions which change or ignore doctrine as needed, the majority of cults that have their origins in America have five important similarities:

1. Outside authority – Bible is not enough
2. Removal of Christ's deity – Jesus is not God
3. Membership in their group necessary to be saved – No hope outside of group
4. Salvation by works – Obedience to group is absolute
5. Christ's atonement is general in nature – Jesus provides opportunity for salvation

We will discuss all of these similarities later in this book.

Cults Are Effective

For a minute, let's just forget about dealing with cults. Instead, let's talk about evangelism. Together, we will form a master plan of evangelism! To formulate our plan, we will grant ourselves unlimited funding. What could we do for God? The sky's the limit! We could give all missionaries full support so that they could work full time to spread the gospel. We could meet people's needs in area of food, family, and housing. We could create jobs and give people purpose, helping them discover their potential. By doing so, we would build the relationships that will allow us to influence them with the gospel! We could produce Christian movies and TV shows, have unlimited advertisements, and support all the struggling Christian radio programs and stations. Wow!

Cults do not have unlimited funding, but many of them have huge incomes in the millions of dollars per day. The kind of discussion described in the previous paragraph might easily occur on a regular basis in their headquarters, with plans developed accordingly.

So let's ask ourselves the question: do we reach people by programs or relationships? The honest answer is that relationships solidify and help stabilize our link with people, but programs can be very effective in generating high levels of responses. The leaders of most cults have come to realize these facts and use them to their advantage. Cults have well-designed initial relationships that later become controlling. For instance, the Mormons have a practice they call "fellowshipping." When I first arrived in Utah, most of the neighbors surrounding my family's home greeted me and gave me gifts of cakes, bread, and fruit. Of course, I was invited to the local Mormon Church or "ward". Do Christians also practice fellowshipping? Yes, we do, but often we are not as efficient at it as the cult organizations are. Unfortunately, sometimes we simply are not as highly motivated.

So why are cults effective? One of the reasons given for cultic motivation in their people is that they have a works salvation, and Christians do not. This need to accomplish their salvation by their actions certainly must be a factor, but it may not be the only reason. Another possibility is the follow-the-leader mentality that is developed in the minds of most cult individuals. Their training shapes their mental processes to let the organization do much of their decision-making for them. When the organization instructs them to reach out to others, they reach out to others. When the organization instructs them to withdraw from others, they withdraw from others.

The answer to cult motivation, however, may be very simple. Ask yourself: what is the driving factor of religious people worldwide? What gives anyone in a works system of salvation the confidence that they are going to receive the highest their religion offers? What supports that kind of mentality? The answer is as old as religion itself: personal pride. When Cain began the first works religion by placing vegetables and fruits, the results of his agricultural effort, on the altar instead of the animal sacrifice that God required, he must have acted with the belief that God would respond favorably. Cain was convinced that what he did was so good that God would adjust His thinking and accept what his human efforts had accomplished. He was motivated by personal pride.

Is using fellowshipping to reach others wrong? Of course not, if it is biblically motivated by a genuine love for the unbeliever. If, however, our motivation centers on earning points before God, doing this activity to please our leadership, or gathering personal trophies for our ministries, then we are no different than the people driven by the cult mentality. We have become cultic ourselves.

Cults Are Evolving

Cults are doctrinally unstable religions. Part of the process of a cult moving to classification as a religion is the stabilization of its doctrines. This process will not ever completely finish, because most cults and religions are based on continual revelation. The fact that a leader in any organization claims that God is giving him or her divine direction opens up the possibility for new practices and concepts. A cult leader once stated that he did not want to know what the dead prophets had said. He only wanted to be told what the living prophet was saying. [2] You don't have to think too hard to realize the powerful control over people that comes with such an approach.

So, here is reality. The doctrines of cults change as needed. If a doctrine has positive results, it can be developed. If it has negative results, it can be changed and then later forgotten. The Mormon doctrine of polygamy was changed by "divine revelation" in the late eighteen hundreds when the US government put pressure on the Latter-day Saints.

A similar revelation took place in 1978, giving African-Americans the right to hold the priesthood in the Mormon Church when social pressure began building against the Mormons. [3] I remember clearly being at Temple Square in Salt Lake City sometime shortly before this "divine revelation" took place. I overheard an elderly white couple talking in upset tones to a Mormon tour guide, wanting to know why black people were not allowed the right of the priesthood. The tour guide was seeking to calm them while avoiding an embarrassing Mormon concept that was believed at that time. This concept taught that one was born into this world with physical characteristics based on how good one was in his/her pre-existence before birth. The lighter the color of hair, eyes, and skin, the better one was at doing good deeds before coming to earth. The darker the hair, eyes, and skin, the more evil an individual had done.

The conversation between the couple and the tour guide continued openly for everyone to hear, until out of desperation the tour guide leaned over and spoke urgently, but softly, "It will be all right. Listen, *we are expecting a revelation!*" Shortly thereafter, the Mormon Church had a revelation, and its doctrine changed – certainly not as a result of this one conversation, but the huge pressure being exerted on the Mormon Church due to changing social influence.

I share this story to point out that any research or book on cults may be out of date before it hits the presses. Therefore, what I am about to state is so important that it will appear several times through this book. Researching cults or religions is interesting, if not fascinating, and may even be helpful in understanding a religious person's worldview, especially his approach to God, but it is not the focus of our preparation to witness to the religious individual about Christ. Remember that, in confronting religious people for our Lord, what the individual believes is what counts, not what the religious system teaches. Christians should invest more time in learning how an individual person thinks than in emphasizing what his leaders teach. After all, the individual will make the final decision concerning what he will accept.

Studying the Bible is the only way to arm ourselves properly for this spiritual battle. The Bible doesn't change, and it has the answers. Because the Bible doesn't change, the answers are always the same.

Purpose of This Book

Let's get to the point. This book is not a book about cult organizations or world religions. We will not review lengthy histories of different religious groups as some books do. Those books are good in their place, but our goal is not a study of historical error. This book is about how to share Christ with individual people who are religious, but lost. This book, then, is a "how to" book. If you want to learn historical facts, plenty of good research material is available. If you want to learn how to witness to religious people, you are now reading a book designed to prepare you to do so.

As frightening as seeing the rise of the "Christian" cults around us is, we have a promise in the midst of it all. When we as biblically born-again believers see these things happen, we know that the coming of Christ is soon. We have read the warnings in Matthew and other places in the New Testament. So the challenge is before us. We need to reach the dear people caught in the trap of a false god and false Christ with the message of the one true God and the biblical Christ. This spiritual rescue is what this book is all about. An important point to remember is that knowing what you believe or why you believe it is not enough. You must know how to communicate it, for without real communication, witnessing is a waste of time!

We are engaged in a real war, fought not with guns but with the weapons of love and the Word of God! Many of the cults claim that they get huge numbers of converts from evangelical Christianity. Alarms should be going off as we ask why. One possible explanation may rest in a historic biblical distinctive known as soul liberty. This precious concept teaches that we have the right to study the Bible ourselves without having to have a church leader interpret the passage for us (1 John 2:27). Our failure is that we believe we have a right to study God's Word without the need of being told what to believe, but then we don't study God's Word. We sadly do not take seriously the spiritual war against evil in which we are enlisted, nor do we truly acknowledge the tragic lost condition of those around us.

Perhaps, however, the real reason cults are successful in convincing evangelical believers to join their cult organizations may be the simple fact that many members of our churches have not experienced biblical salvation. These church members use Christian terms for which they have created personal definitions which are not biblical but which satisfy their own understanding. This individualism makes them vulnerable to persuasive arguments from other religions, especially the redefining of terms the cults practice so well.

This book is designed to help you witness to religious people of all types. Many of the experiences and examples will deal with Mormonism, for I have been learning how to communicate Christ to these dear people for many years. My wife and I spent eighteen years in Utah as missionaries establishing a church in a city that was ninety-five percent Mormon. The only other two alternatives that existed in that city were a Jehovah's Witness Kingdom Hall and a Hare Krishna compound. We always had opportunities to share Christ!

The variables in witnessing to cults and religions are nearly infinite. Even so, once an individual has learned to witness to one of these groups, he can potentially witness to all of them. The principles used in witnessing are interchangeable, remaining basically the same. They are interchangeable because they are not based on what the cults or religions believe, but on what the Bible says.

The material for this book comes from the many seminars on witnessing to religious people that the Lord has allowed me to give in churches, schools, and colleges across the country and in other places in the world. I have received many requests to put what I have shared in writing. The result is before you. May the Lord accomplish His purpose through these pages.

One final thought: this book is not intended to be an exhaustive theological study of the doctrines it discusses. Instead, we will focus on individual verses and passages, reviewing what is being said and how to use them so that real communication will result. When a person is involved in a discussion with a religious individual, he does not have time to explain a whole system of theology. He needs tangible reasons found in straightforward biblical statements for what he believes. Now with this condition understood, let's get started.

One

Proper Attitudes

I remember wanting to do something different during the summer of my seventeenth year. I had told the Lord when I was ten that I was willing to be a missionary for Him. At the time, being a missionary meant going to Africa, not that I had any particular draw to Africa, but as most of the missionaries I knew were going to Africa, I figured I would end up there, too. As I prayed, inquiring of the Lord what He would have me do that summer, the pastor of the church I was attending asked if I would be interested in serving on a short-term mission trip in Utah. He shared with me that I would be witnessing to Mormons. My response was simple. I did not know what a Mormon was, but if he was lost, I would witness to him. So I sent off my application and was approved. I received a packet in the mail filled with information about Mormonism. I went into shock as I studied their doctrine. I thought: *Wow! This stuff is better than science fiction!* So I packed my Bible and some research books and headed to Utah to set the Mormons straight on biblical truth.

My home church wanted to help me; so they bought me a bus ticket for the twelve-hundred-mile trip west. I don't know if you have ever ridden on a bus that far, but please do not believe the words on the side of the bus that say express! We traveled for miles, stopping at every little town along the way. About halfway to Utah, the bus stopped, and a pretty young lady about my age stepped onto the bus and – to my delight and surprise – sat down next to me. I remember thinking: *This trip is going to be all right!* We chatted for a bit, and then I asked her where she was headed. She told me she was going out west to visit some relatives. She then asked me the same question. I replied that I was on my way to Utah to be a missionary to the Mormons.

"Oh, really," she responded. "Why would you want to do that?"

You must understand that at the age of seventeen, I had a lot of tact – NOT! I replied, "I am going to Utah to reach that hideous cult with the message of Christ."

She smiled and flashed those pretty eyes at me and said, "I'm a Mormon."

Oops, I thought. *Oh, well, I've got one now; I might as well witness to her.* So I started witnessing. To my surprise, she started witnessing back. I gave it everything I had. I pulled no punches. Neither did she. As the miles rolled by, I noticed that passengers who had been sitting around us were getting farther and farther toward the back of the bus. At lunch times, the girl and I would eat together and continue our intense debate.

Somewhere in Wyoming, the flu bug hit me, and I became very sick. This Mormon girl got a paper towel, dampened it with water, and placed it on my forehead. When the bus stopped, she went to a drugstore and bought me some medicine. This care and attention was embarrassing. I was trying to save her soul, and she was being nice to me! She got off the bus one stop before me, and I have not seen her since. I know the story would be more dramatic had I married her, but that kind of fairy tale is not what happened.

God, however, got His point across. Here I was going to Utah to wage war on the Mormons. Instead, God put me in contact with a kind Mormon girl. He certainly knows how to soften a guy's heart. God taught me through this young lady that Mormons are not the stupid, blind, religious kooks we often associate with cults. Instead, they are real people with real feelings, hopes, and desires. We are in this spiritual battle not against cultic or religious people, but on their behalf.

Neither is the war against any cult organizations or religions. For instance, if someone discovered something historical that proved the Mormon Church wrong and their whole religious system collapsed, millions of Mormons would not flock to hear the gospel. Instead, two possibilities would likely happen. First, many Mormons would probably join other cults. With the follow-the-leader mentality that cults have, transferring to another cult would be an easier move than might be expected. I am convinced, however, that a large number of Mormons would become agnostic. For many of them, their whole lives have centered on their religion, and once it was gone, the confidence that God existed would be gone with it. I have seen that scenario played out on a small scale when Mormons became convinced that Mormonism was wrong. For some of them, all hope was gone. Let's face it. If a large cult was discredited, then millions of its members would soon find themselves either in other cults or in a state of disillusionment. Incidentally, the chances of anything successfully destroying a large cult are almost zero. Many archeological finds have contradicted Mormonism without much reaction from the Mormon people.

Blind faith is powerful. For that reason, people need the supernatural light of God's Word to see! Therefore, our mission is not to destroy cults or religions; our mission is to reach individual members of cults or religions with the personal message of Christ.

Witnessing with an Attitude

A person's attitude often affects what he thinks of others and what they think of him. In the area of witnessing, especially when witnessing to someone who holds a strong religious conviction, a person's attitude can determine whether a conversation will end on friendly or unfriendly terms. An argument can greatly damage the cause of Christ, and repairing that damage may take years of work. We will spend some serious time in this book on how to talk to religious people without becoming angry, but first, let's look at another issue that prevents successful witnessing.

Some Christians believe that we should not even try to talk to cult individuals. Before we go any further in our discussion, we need to understand the reasons why some Christians do not witness to cults, and on the other hand, why we should.

"The Bible tells me not to."

This response may be a biblical attempt to justify not having to deal with the cults at all. Why would anyone hold such a position? The answer is that they believe that some verses in the Bible teach us not to allow any false teachers into our homes (2 John 9-10).

What about 2 John 9-10? Do these verses allow or forbid a conversation to occur in our homes with a member of the cults? The verses read: "Whosoever transgresseth, and abideth not in the doctrine of Christ, hath not God. He that abideth in the doctrine of Christ, he hath both the Father and the Son. If there come any unto you, and bring not this doctrine, receive him not into your house, neither bid him God speed."

First, we need to recognize that good men are on both sides of this issue concerning whether we should let a member of the cults into our homes. Whatever we believe these verses to mean, we must ask ourselves this question: is the intent of these verses to give the believer an excuse to not witness to the cults? 1 Peter 3:15 challenges us to "be ready always to give an answer to every man." So whether we believe we can let them into our house or we believe they must remain at our door, Peter still challenges us to share Christ with them. Being alert to the situation, however, is important. If a believer is a new Christian or is unsure of what to say or what he believes, then delaying the conversation until that believer has had some time to study and prepare may be wise. (In the meantime, the young believer could give his visitor good literature that shares biblical truths and does not attack the religion of the person to whom he is talking, if the cult individual will accept it.) Building confidence in using the Bible to witness may take awhile, but every Christian should make continual effort in this area. The Bible is the only earthly object available that has the supernatural power to get the job done.

We should always seek to be as ready as possible, but we should remember that most believers, including those of us who have witnessed to cult individuals for years, will never feel fully prepared. Fully knowing or anticipating another person's beliefs is impossible. That lack is where God comes in. Witnessing to religious people demands trust that God will be with us. Understanding this fact, we all need to prepare, but we dare not make the mistake of waiting forever to get started witnessing.

I have heard the suggestion that, if a family has young children at an impressionable age, the parents may want to consider setting an appointment with the cult representatives and sending the children to Grandma's for the evening, unless, of course, Grandma's a Jehovah's Witness, which might complicate the situation a little. Having the children present, however, may be an advantage. They will begin to learn that false religions exist in the world and that sharing the truth with religious people in a loving way is important. If parents decide to have their children sit in on witnessing opportunities, they must take time to talk to their children afterward so that they do not become confused. This time of deprogramming should be taken seriously!

The reason why someone in Christian leadership would tend to want to interpret the 2 John passage as prohibiting talking to the cults is easy to understand. Protecting the people in our churches from error is easier if we do not have to worry about them talking to cults in their homes. The question is: does God want us to hold such a position, even for safety's sake?

The following are reasons why I believe this position should not be held:

1. We are commanded to be always ready to witness to everyone (1 Peter 3:15). Instead of Christian leadership telling people that they do not have to witness, we need to be training them how to do so. So we leaders first need to learn that skill for ourselves.

2. If 2 John 9-10 means what some say it does, then in order to be consistent, we would have to refuse access to our homes not only to religious leaders, but also to all unbelievers.

3. The best way to win someone to Christ is to become his friend, including inviting him into

our home. This tactic is being used on a regular basis all across the country and on foreign fields as well.

4. As we discussed earlier, the danger to people in our churches may very well rest in the fact that many of them may not be saved (1 John 2:19). We need to re-teach the gospel message seriously again and again to the people in our churches.

So what does 2 John 9-10 teach? We can understand this passage in several ways without implying that we cannot witness to cult members in our homes. First, some theologians believe that 2 John was written to a local church and the sister churches it had started (i.e., "the elect lady and her children" in verse 1). If so, then John was saying not to allow false teachers in the house of God or have them conduct church services. Therefore, the verse would not apply to our personal homes. Whether by interpretation of the verse in this fashion or application of the biblical principle of not being subject to those who teach wrongly, we should never allow false teachers to come into our homes to instruct us. This injunction does not mean that we cannot allow them to come into our homes with the purpose of witnessing to them. We can see a major difference in intention!

Some Bible students base a second possible position on the fact that all kinds of traveling teachers sought audiences in the days of John the Apostle. Some were good, and some were bad. The custom was for a traveling teacher to find a home out of which to base his ministry. If John was talking about this custom, he was saying not to give teachers of false doctrine a place to stay or encourage them in their work ("bid him Godspeed"). This interpretation should not, however, lead to the conclusion that we are to forsake those with physical needs who do not agree with us. We may help any individual in need if we do so with the purpose of showing God's love and reaching that one for Jesus Christ, but we are also to be wise enough not to support false ministries. Giving a cup of cool water in a moment of godly compassion is certainly different than providing that water to a false teacher in order to sustain his ability to carry out his mission. One action fulfils loving even our enemies, while the other supports error.

Whatever position you conclude is biblical, the main principle the passage clearly teaches is to be able to recognize error, reject it, and at no time have a submissive attitude to false doctrine. Again, we need to take seriously our need of Bible study before we tackle error (1 Peter 3:15). This necessity does not excuse us from witnessing if we do not know the Bible. It prompts us to get ready and learn the Bible! If you conclude that you should not let a member of the cults into your house, then plan to witness to this person as you stand at your door. After all, we are commanded to share Christ!

"You can't win them anyway!"

I have heard this second excuse given many times as a reason not to witness to cults. After all, you hear of very few cult individuals getting saved. The fact is that, for most people involved in cults, the way out is very difficult. We must realize that people usually do not change their positions after just one discussion, especially if those positions have been held for years and are sincerely believed. God told the prophet Ezekiel that he was being sent to a people who would not listen, but he was to go anyway (Ezekiel 2:3-5). Why? God wanted the message shared, even if no one responded. We have a responsibility to share Christ with cult and other religious individuals, even if no one listens.

Most important of all, we must remember that we do not change people; the Holy Spirit does. The real burden of reaching these people for Christ rests with God. We do not prove God is right; we merely share what is right. Truth is truth no matter what. When we cannot lead someone to the truth, we must realize that we have not failed; the one who does not accept the truth has experienced the failure that comes from the deceptiveness of sin. Mentioning failure brings us to our next point.

"I am afraid of not knowing an answer or failing God."

I have often heard this third excuse that people give not to witness to cults. Again, we must realize that the truth of God does not rise or fall on us (Psalm 100:5). God does not go into a panic in heaven when our mind goes blank and we find ourselves unable to respond to error! We have to learn to trust the Lord to enable our minds to do the job. Not knowing answers should challenge us to find the answers. Although we need to be responsible and train our minds, ultimately, either God fights for us, or we cannot win.

Frightened? The Mormon missionary handbook informs the Mormon missionary not to be afraid when he presents what he believes to others. Why? The handbook goes on to share that the people to whom he is talking are as frightened as he is. So how do we handle fear? We must accept the fact that fear is a natural result of feeling threatened, and witnessing can be a very threatening experience. Knowing the promises in God's Word will help us as we seek to serve Him. Listen to what God told Judah in Isaiah 41:10. "Fear thou not; for I am with thee: be not dismayed; for I am thy God: I will strengthen thee; yea, I will help thee; yea, I will uphold thee with the right hand of my righteousness." Either God keeps His promises, or witnessing has no value. Why would we want to introduce people to a God who lies?

Nature of Religion

Two words are vital in understanding what can be to most of us the complicated process of witnessing to the religious mind. The first word is "emotion". Emotion is one of the ruling forces in religion, if not the major one. When man lost the righteous relationship with God that he had enjoyed in the Garden of Eden, a great void appeared in human existence. People have sought to fill this emptiness through experience, relationships, accomplishments, and especially religion. Throughout the world, religions that are monumentally different in doctrine have this one unique characteristic in common. They seek to fill the emptiness of human life with experiential fulfillment, usually in the realm of emotion.

Even those religious individuals who desire to control and suppress emotion experience the emotional results of such attempts. For most religions, although not all, the God experience becomes visual through images of religious worship, such as cathedrals, statues, and ritual services. Alongside this visual experience is the physical realm of religion through touch or taste, the smell of incense, or hearing of lofty music. Religion may take the form of experiencing self-denial and suffering, leaving the individual with a self-righteous sense of personal holiness. The emotional sensation of personal religious pride and personal religious humility becomes the central goal. And this sensation temporarily satisfies the emptiness. The true experience of knowing God, however, is a tough act to follow, and all of the emotional tapestry of religion can never permanently meet the human need of God.

At this moment in our discussion, some readers may be thinking that I am trying to remove emotion from the worship of God. Nothing could be further from the truth. Knowing the true God of the Bible is an emotional experience unparalleled in any other human experience. It should be enjoyed and appreciated; the focus, however, must not be on the emotional experience of worship, but on the God we are worshiping.

This distinction brings us to the second key word in dealing with the religious mind, and that word is "truth". I would like to use a very simple illustration to share the importance of this concept. If I wanted to be able to recognize whether a stick was crooked when I saw it, I could take two different approaches. One, I could apply for a government grant to research crooked sticks. Then I could travel around the world collecting specimens of crooked sticks. I could put great effort into cataloging and identifying each of the different classifications of twists and angles. OR – I could study a straight stick. Then every time I came across a stick, I would compare it to the straight one and immediately know if the stick was crooked or straight. Why? Because crooked can take many different, almost infinite, forms. Straight will always be straight. Truth is like the straight stick, and error is like the crooked stick. Error can take many different, almost infinite, forms. Truth will always be truth. Truth is the same today as it was yesterday, and it will be the same tomorrow. To deal with religion in its multitude of forms, we must continually maintain that truth is absolute, communicable through the written word, and in fact, knowable. Truth is truth no matter what. We must realize that truth does not rise or fall on debate, nor is it dependent on our words. We want to be as skilled as possible in communication, but God's truth will still remain intact even if we do not convince someone who is wrong of what is right.

To comprehend the issue better, we need to understand the nature of truth. It is neither abstract nor relative. Not only in cults but also in many religions around the world, truth is not regarded as absolute. To many religions, as well as to the people within them, truth shifts as needed and becomes what is desired of it. But real truth is absolute by nature. To believe in real truth, one has to believe in a consistent, universal reality. This concept states that only one reality that is the same for all exists. In the world of human religion and reason, real truth is not allowed to exist. To state that one truth applies to all is intolerant to the mind of human reasoning and to the thought processes of religious unity. Even though many cults teach that they have absolute authority, their absolute truth changes to match their needs.

God did not create truth. Instead, God is an absolute Being who exists in absolute reality defined by absolute truths. Truth is not an object to be shaped and developed but an aspect of reality that does not evolve or change. Real truth has many benefits to it. One case in point is morality. Real truth will produce consistent, fair morality. Consistent, fair morality is the result of a loving, holy, consistent God who exists in the realm of real truth. This consistent morality must universally apply to everyone if its existence is based on real truth. Otherwise, morality is relative, serving the individual who claims to believe it instead of directing him. Either there is totally consistent morality, or there is no morality. Once morality is no longer thought to be absolute, it is disassociated from real truth and becomes something else, with nothing to which it can anchor. If there is no real morality, then morality is established by the most powerful. This logic explains why religious leaders (including many who claim to be Christian) and sects have killed and maimed around the world. Their understanding of God and truth allowed them to act with an inconsistent morality, because real truth did not exist for them.

God is more than just the most powerful Being imposing His will on others. The God of the Bible is good, and He does what is right. The biblical history of God's interaction with man, especially in the area of redemption, demonstrates that God will not act contrary to moral right, even at the cost of His Son.

But what about the immoral acts that Christians in human history have done in the name of God? These Christians did not have a biblical view of God! Any view of God that changes moral rules so that they apply to one group and not another or apply to some people but not others does not come from the Bible. These views come from misunderstanding the Bible. This discussion opens a whole new area that does not fit within the parameters of this book. The key to our immediate discussion is remembering that truth is not variable but absolute, consistent, and knowable.

Cults and Conflicts

As just stated, in the heat of spiritual battle, we must remember that we do not have to convince anyone of the truth; that burden is the responsibility of the Holy Spirit (John 16:7-11). Will I ever grow tired of saying that fact? NO! Why? We all tend to drop into survival mode when the pressure is on. When we need God the most, we are usually trying to do the job without Him. Sometimes the problem is as simple as forgetting that the Holy Spirit does not have to do all His work in a one-hour discussion. We do not want the cult individual to get away without hearing the gospel! We may find ourselves thinking: *This may be my only opportunity to share Christ with this person. I've got to give him everything I can from the Bible.* Or worse yet, maybe other believers are sitting in on the conversation, and we feel that if we do not win this battle of words, they will not respect us or our ability with the Bible.

Those who witness to people in religions and cults commonly agree that leading such individuals to the biblical Christ usually takes many years. So a multitude of Christians will probably be witnessing to each religious person along the way. I think we all would enjoy being the final one, the one who leads that individual to the Lord. Being the fourth or the sixteenth or the twenty-second person and not seeing the end result is tough. The truth is that most of us will not see people responding the way we would like to see them respond when it comes to witnessing to religious individuals; yet we must not grow discouraged.

I remember speaking in a church in Iowa and having some Mormon missionaries show up to see what I had to say. Afterward, I spent quite a long time talking with them. One of the two, the quiet one, started asking a lot of questions. Clearly, he had an open mind concerning the Bible. We kept in contact for a few days, but then the Mormon Church sent him somewhere else, rather unexpectedly in fact. Later, I met an elderly lady in another part of the country who knew this young Mormon missionary. She had been witnessing to him before I ever met him. The Mormon leaders had pulled him out of her area and sent him to where I was! We must believe that God is in control and knows what He is doing!

Because of our limited vision, the easiest thing to do in a discussion with a cult individual may be to charge in and prove that we are not cowards. However, to remain silent and polite when someone else twists our words or changes his position in midstream takes real courage. One method of witnessing used today suggests, when confronting a person of the cults, that you should draw your sword (figuratively, I hope), attack incorrect history, slice and dice false leadership, and then put together a Christian from the shattered pieces. Personally, I believe that this concept is not biblical; so I challenge you not to use it! There is a place for the examination of historical error and deceptive leadership, but we must remember that only the Word of God gives life to the spiritual dead. Only a being with spiritual life can understand spiritual truth. We may destroy a cult individual's belief in his organization's history and leaders, but we need to be extremely careful that we do not create a bitter resentfulness to God in the process. This religious system may well be all that he knows of God. Once his belief in the system is destroyed, his belief in God may be destroyed. He may even come to the conclusion that, if God exists, He certainly is not trustworthy.

Leaving the discussion on friendly terms is more important than saying everything one might want to say and departing as enemies. At this point, you may be thinking: *Wow, I've really blown it with cult people!* Don't let the past discourage you. If any of us have used the attack method in the past and now regret it, we should remember what Paul said in Philippians 3:13 about "forgetting those things which are behind," and start out fresh with a new approach. We have a beautiful promise in Romans 8:28 that God can take anything, including any approach to witnessing, and use it for good. Leave the past with Him.

Some of those reading this book may have developed their skills through the years, and they may be very adept at pointing out what is wrong with a cult (in written literature and historical actions) and then leading the cult individual to Christ. My intent is not to condemn or criticize them. I praise God for anyone who is saved from religious quicksand, and I am thankful for those individuals who are involved in the rescue. May God continue to use them, even if their method is different than what I believe God would have me use.

Right Tools

In order to witness to people who are in error regarding what God has said, two important areas must function within the person witnessing. They are, in a preparation sense, the right tools for the job. The first tool is the love of God, and the second one is knowledge of the Bible. One without the other will be ineffective. A person may have knowledge of the Bible but lack love, and he will only succeed in driving people away. Another may have love but lack knowledge of the Bible, so that not only will he be unable to share the truth but he, himself, may even become confused as to what the truth is.

Love of God

In John 13:34 we read the words of Christ: "A new commandment I give unto you, That ye love one another; as I have loved you, that ye also love one another." In a very real sense, Christians have forgotten how to love. We must understand that love is the key to reaching people for Christ. Paul wrote in 2 Corinthians 5:14 that "the love of Christ constraineth us." People wonder at the cults and their apparent zeal in spreading their faith. As we shared earlier, what we often forget is that cult members must witness to other people because they believe that witnessing is one of the works they have to do to get to heaven or receive God's best, which may be different than the heaven of the Bible. True Christians believe that biblical salvation is accomplished by Christ alone apart from their works (Ephesians 2:8-9). Therefore, if we share the message of Christ, we do so not because we have to but because we want to. We do so because of love. At least, love is the reason we should do so. This motivation does not diminish the fact that Christ commanded us to witness. In fact, our love for Christ supports and encourages our obedience to His command. Because we love Him, we keep His commandments. We do not keep His commandments in order to love Him. We keep His commandments because we love Him. Our love for the unsaved is not what motivates us, but our love for Christ. Even when the unsaved act cruelly and disrespectfully to us, our love does not change, for it is focused on Christ.

In John 13:35, Jesus states: "By this shall all men know that ye are my disciples, if ye have love one to another." Notice that the world will not know you are a disciple of Christ because you go to church or because you have been baptized or because you live a good, clean Christian life. Why not? Certainly these things are important. When one goes to church, he is in an organized study program of God's Word, and he enjoys fellowship with other believers. When one is baptized, he is following the biblical way of publicly identifying himself with Christ. When one lives a moral life, he is protecting himself and his Christian testimony. Yet, Jesus said that one's love would let the world know that a person belongs to Him. Why? The answer is that a whole world full of religious people out there goes to church, gets baptized, and leads moral lives. Something has to be different about us, and that something different is our love.

For instance, people in cults are capable of reaching out to others outside their group in a very positive way. Remember the Mormon term, fellow-shipping, as well as the previous statement that cults have well-designed initial relationships that later become controlling. The truth is that loving the cult individual is not the love that will successfully bring him out of his religion. He was probably brought into his religion because members of that cult reached lovingly out to him when others did not. So what kind of love was Jesus discussing? Let us read the verse again. "By this shall all men know that ye are my disciples, if ye have love one to another" (John 13:35). How we love the unsaved cult person will not be what will stand out to him. He expects us to reach out to him in love. He does the same to others. What will catch his attention is how we reflect the love of God to each other within the church. Because cults become controlling once you join their organization and because conditional love is used by cult leaders to manipulate people within their group, Christians loving each other unconditionally will stand out, clearly demonstrating that we possess real truth. Oops! Do we stand out? Do we love each other unconditionally within our churches? Sadly, many churches have become cultic in the way that they control and manipulate people instead of reflecting Christ as they were meant to do. No wonder we do not reach people caught in religious error. We are no different.

Even though our love for each other will be the most effective testimony to a religious individual, we certainly still want to extend the love of Christ to him also. Once I knocked on a door in Utah, and a Mormon lady answered. I told her I was from the local Baptist church, and she informed me that she was going to slam the door in my face. When I inquired why, she told me that, when her son had been on his mission, a Baptist had slammed the door in his face, and she was going to slam the door in mine. I told her that seemed fair to me; so she slammed the door. Please do not slam the door in anyone's face. Have an attitude of love. If you do not know what to say when the cults come, be polite and explain that you cannot talk now. Later in the book, we'll give some suggestions concerning what to do if you are not ready to talk, but for now, remember the word "polite". When the cult leaves, call your pastor for advice, and then study!

Some people have a "two tract rack" attitude. We have one type of tract for people like the mailman or the average individual we meet, with titles like "What Must I Do to Be Saved?" or "God Loves You!" Then we have the other tract rack for the cults. The titles in this tract rack could be "Why Jehovah's Witnesses Are Not Witnesses of Jehovah!" or "Why Was Mary Baker Eddy off Her Rocker?" Hopefully not! By the way, these last two titles were made up, but....

Picture this situation. A couple of Mormon missionaries arrive at our door. We greet them, and then we hand them a tract titled, let's say, "Why Was Joseph Smith a False Prophet?" They surely must be excited about receiving it! After all, it is the truth! From now on, they will listen to everything we have to say, right? Wrong! We have most likely lost their interest, and no doubt they are just looking for a way to leave as soon as possible! So find good tracts that give the way of salvation and define the terms they use. The problem that exists with many tracts available today is that they are written with the assumption that the readers know what the words "saved" or "Christian," as well as other terms, mean. Find a tract that explains what salvation is and how to receive it. Be cautious in giving a tract that criticizes a person's religion or the founder of that religion. Use material that presents the positive aspects of the Bible and what it teaches.

Knowledge of the Bible

To know every doctrine of every cult or religion is impossible. First, simply too many of them are in the world. Secondly, as we pointed out earlier, their doctrines are constantly changing. We cannot keep up, but we must not give up! Again, studying other books about cults is not wrong, but knowing the Bible prepares us for anything that Satan can throw at us.

Suppose we looked out the window and saw some Jehovah's Witnesses coming down the street. We immediately grab the cult book we purchased for just such an occasion and quickly study the section on Jehovah's Witnesses. They finally arrive at our door, and we are ready! They begin talking, and we immediately point out some historical inconsistency of their past along with some strange doctrine that they believe. They respond by ignoring the historical issue and claiming that they do not believe the strange doctrine. We respond by showing them the evidence from our book on cults. Stunned by our presentation, they acknowledge that we are right, and we discover that we have convinced them that this doctrine we have brought up is really part of their beliefs. What have we succeeded in doing? We have taught them a doctrinal class in their religion, and now they better understand what they believe!

It should go without saying that we do not want to teach members of a religion their doctrine when they do not know it! Instead, we should deal with what the individual member of that religion believes, not what his organization teaches, and then, understanding his personal religion as he sees it, center our discussion on the Bible!

This strategy brings us to an important question: do you believe what you believe because you have read it in the Bible? Or do you believe it because someone has told you it is in the Bible? There is the challenge. Setting aside time for concentrated Bible study will be hard work, especially if you work a forty-hour-a-week job or more, but it is worthwhile. As God has taken the time to tell us about Himself in the Bible, let us not content ourselves with settling for a second opinion. Let us hear firsthand from Him in His recorded Word!

So here we are at the inescapable conclusion again: knowledge of what the Bible teaches is crucial! We cannot get away from this fact. Peter brings it to our attention once more in that troubling verse, 1 Peter 3:15, where we are told to "be ready always to give an answer to every man that asketh you a reason of the hope that is in you." Notice, however, that the verse says to be ready to answer the man that asks. Peter doesn't mean that we shouldn't initiate conversations, only that we cannot make people want to know the truth. God has to put into their hearts a desire to listen. We can never convince the closed mind, but we need to be ready to share when God opens the door. Oh, yes, we should finish the verse: "with meekness and fear." Not only should we be ready to share the truth, we must do so with a humble spirit. God has opened our eyes by His grace. We have no reason for pride.

Finally, we must realize that, in dealing with religious people and especially the cults, we are going to come across some strange concepts, ideas, and stories. Centering on these aberrancies will be a great temptation, but resist doing so. The standard by which we are to judge whether any belief system is right or wrong is not that it's strange or has strange ideas, but that its position contradicts the Bible. The Bible will forever be the line God has drawn in the sand.

Two

Friendly Discussions

Y ou will meet them, maybe at the airport or bus station, perhaps as a fellow employee at work, possibly when you greet your neighbor in the morning, maybe even the mechanic repairing your car, or simply when the doorbell rings while you're reading the paper, but you will meet them. What do you do when a Mormon, a Jehovah's Witness, or someone belonging to another cult or false religion comes to your door or into your life? What do you say? "Ah - hello. I can't talk now, but our pastor lives down the street, the third house on the right. He'd have a better chance of converting you than I." Of course not! But what do you say?

The answer to that question is what the next few chapters are all about. Knowing how to respond in this kind of witnessing opportunity is important. What you are about to read is by no means an exact procedure, but a basic outline to follow and adapt to each situation. We have no magic formulas, but we do have good principles that are biblically based. We need to discover what they are.

Opening Comments

Many witnessing situations take place on neutral territory in the public or social arenas. Usually, both individuals (the person witnessing and the person being witnessed to) are on equal footing. This situation is true unless one is in a politically or religiously controlled location. The neutral territory doesn't mean that witnessing anywhere is easy, but witnessing can be very challenging when one is in a potentially hostile environment, where comfort and safety is removed. In all evangelism efforts, a common sense of discomfort comes when someone is knocking on someone else's door. This situation places the would-be evangelist at the disadvantage of being in someone else's territory, socially requiring politeness. Perhaps the most positive situation in which to witness is when someone comes to our homes and wants to tell us what they believe. This situation often causes the most fear, even though it is the best and easiest opportunity to witness because it is our home and we are in control. I can, however, almost certainly guarantee that it will be the most inconvenient! Religious people seem to show up at our door when everything is going wrong, from children crying to plumbing not working. We have to ask ourselves the question: how much do I really want to witness to lost people?

So what do we do when the religious or cultic person comes knocking? Again, when cult members or religious people approach us in our home, we must remember that it is our home and that we do have the right to control the situation. We must not let any self-assured manner fool us. They know they are guests, and ultimately they must respect our wishes.

The following scenario is based on a visit to our home by a cult individual. Keep in mind that the basic principles will be the same in any witnessing situation where we encounter a religious person, whether at our home or somewhere else. When such an individual comes to our door, we might begin the conversation like this: "I appreciate your coming by and wanting to share with me what you believe. I enjoy nothing more than discussing the Bible and what it has to say. I would like to share something with you first, if I may. I've seen some Bible discussions turn into debates and arguments. Neither person listened to the other because the person who was supposed to be listening was thinking about what he was going to say next. I'm not interested in a debate. What I do enjoy is a discussion based on the priority of truth. You see, I want to know the truth of God above everything else. I want to know it above being a Baptist or a Mormon or a Catholic or any other religious denomination. If you share something from the Bible with me that I've never seen before, I promise you that I'll study the Bible again and examine what you present. Then we can get together again and discuss it. At the same time, if I should show you something from the Bible you have never seen before, you should be willing to study it also, and then we can discuss it when we get back together later."

Under normal circumstances, saying what is written in the previous paragraph word for word is probably impractical; besides, quoting something memorized would be unnatural. What we want to do is get the basic idea of where to head with the conversation. We are not engaged in a contest to see who can outtalk the other person; we are engaged in a search for what God has said.

Remember three important concepts:
1. Seek the truth together
2. No debate
3. Time to review

Seek the truth together!
The challenge we want to put before the person to whom we are witnessing is that truth is more important than defending our denominational affiliation. I know and understand that most Christians do not view cults as part of a Christian denomination, but many cults see themselves that way. The point simply is not worth spending the time arguing about. We have more important issues to address. The following must become clear to the person to whom we are witnessing: the priority of our lives must be the truth of God. We should be willing to change what we believe if God's Word teaches something different from our views! How can we expect others to change if we do not have a submissive spirit to God in this area? Christians must become truth-driven people if we expect others to accept biblical truth. Certainly, we need to know what the Bible says

so that we do not become confused by false doctrine, but our discussion with others must center on truth and not personal belief.

No debate!

We do not argue anyone into heaven. Conclusions in discussions should not be based on who is the best with words. Truth does not change if one individual outtalks another. Our goal should not be to win the argument with the person with whom we are talking. Our goal should be to communicate Christ to this fellow human being to the best of our ability. Respect is an important part of witnessing which the individual will probably remember long after the doctrine we have presented is forgotten. This attitude keeps the opportunity to share Christ possible for the next Christian God brings into this religious person's life.

Will being polite while someone else interrupts and cuts us off be easy? No, I am afraid that good behavior can be very difficult to maintain when it is not reciprocated. Being respectful, however, honors God. But are we compromising by not getting the last word? No, we can be certain that God will get the last word! Will acting respectfully guarantee that we will not upset people? Not at all! People will get upset when they encounter the Word of God and it disagrees with them. An important point to remember is to be certain that the individual with whom we are talking is upset at the Bible, not at the disrespectful way we presented it to him.

Time to review!

Knowing every doctrine of every religion and every cult is impossible. The more one witnesses to religious people, the more certain one is of this fact. Each religious individual we encounter will have his or her view of religion, and millions of religious people are in our world. Someone somewhere will surprise us with a concept we have not heard before. Therefore, a time to review is very important, for it takes the pressure off all people in the conversation and also challenges each one to take time to study what has been discussed. Remember, rarely are religious people reached in one session.

If at any time during the discussion we realize that tempers are rising, we need to be honest and share what we sense happening. We should be able to tell those to whom we are talking honestly that God is honored by a respectful discussion and apologize if we have acted incorrectly by becoming angry. Having a fellow believer with us when we witness is almost always an encouragement, and he or she can help in sensing the atmosphere of the conversation. A husband and wife together sharing Christ can be quite effective.

Discussion Principles

Simply put, we could discuss many principles for witnessing, but here are three that have proven very effective in guiding interaction not only with religious people but also with anyone who does not know the God of the Bible. These principles are not chronological concepts to be covered in a step-by-step manner. Instead, they are like three horses pulling a chariot together side by side. All three of these principles should be used through the conversation at the same time. Here is the list:

1. Establish authority
2. Define terms
3. Focus on salvation

Biblical authority will most certainly be in the forefront of any discussion, because it sets the basis for the rest of the discussion. The issues of biblical authority, however, will always be present throughout the conversation and will most likely be discussed repeatedly. Terminology will always be an issue, because communication requires words. Ultimately, salvation by its nature and importance must be our focus.

If I were to give a test at the end of this book, one of the questions I would ask of you would be to list these three principles and describe how they guide the discussion. Of course, the real test is when members of a cult sit down in your living room and you must meet the challenge of sharing Christ with them. That challenge, of course, is the one we all face.

Establish Authority

The authority to determine truth and error is very important. When someone is tried in a courtroom, the law determines whether what that person did is right or wrong. When witnessing to cult members, as we are dealing with what God has said, a final authority must be set up between the two parties to settle any dispute. No discussion is profitable if conclusions are reached based upon opinions. The important point is what God has said about the subject under discussion.

For the biblical Christian, the only authority that he can accept is the Bible, but in the world of cults, many authorities reign besides the Bible. Establishing the Bible as our authority is a simple statement of fact. Helping the individual with whom we are talking to reach the same conclusion often is much more difficult. One of the most common reasons cults give for the right of their existence is that the Bible has errors, or at least that it cannot be understood without help. The cults claim that they are the ones who correct the errors and help others understand. In other words, cults exist on authority outside the Bible. Their approach to the Bible can be demonstrated in the following three statements:

"The Bible has errors, and you need our corrections."

"The Bible cannot be understood without our leaders' interpretation."

"The Bible is not complete, and you need our additional scriptures."

Mormons, for instance, have many authorities. They have the *Book of Mormon*, the *Pearl of Great Price*, the *Doctrine and Covenants*, the Bible (as far as it is, in their opinion, translated correctly), "a living prophet," twelve apostles, what they call the priesthood, and finally, they believe they themselves are receiving revelation. As the *Book of Mormon, Doctrine and Covenants,* and *Pearl of Great Price* are all written in a very similar style to the King James Version of the Bible, Mormons can use verses that sound like they are from the King James Bible to prove their position, until they are asked for a reference. Then the Christian discovers that the verses are from 2 Nephi or the Book of Abraham. Mormons are not the only ones who use authority other than the Bible, but they are certainly among the most outspoken about the practice. Many of the other groups hide behind the idea that they have the correct interpretation of the Bible.

Bible Claims Authority

In 2 Timothy 3:15-16 we read, "And that from a child thou hast known the holy scriptures, which are able to make thee wise unto salvation through faith which is in Christ Jesus. All scripture is given by inspiration of God, and is profitable for doctrine, for reproof, for correction, for instruction in righteousness." I will not take space at this time to give the biblical reasons for accepting the Bible and the Bible alone as our authority. A whole section in this book is devoted to that purpose. What is important to note is that the Bible makes a clear claim to be the accurate authority in all on which it comments. To the best of our ability, we must learn how to demonstrate that it is the sole authority in a particular conversation with someone who is most likely not convinced.

Bible Cult

The words "Bible cult" conjure up a paradox in the Christian's mind, and I am aware of that fact. I have chosen to use this term to refer to those groups that accept the Bible in some form but believe doctrine contradictory to the fundamental concepts of biblical Christianity. (I suppose the term "Bible religion" could be used to identify those groups that are not listed as cults but teach false doctrine.) Paul wrote about false religious individuals appearing as true believers in 2 Corinthians 11:2-4, 13-15 when he stated that they follow a different Christ (in reality, Satan), have false apostles, and appear able to do works of outward righteousness. Because these groups believe in the Bible (although they may have an incorrect view of it), the person sharing Christ with them has a starting point whereby he can establish the sole authority of the Bible.

So what can we as Bible believers use as the starting point for discussion with those who claim to believe in the Bible but do not hold the same view about God's Book? The answer is to share a simple truth. Based on the premise that the Bible alone is our authority, discussion logically must be limited to the Bible, because it is the only authority we accept. Any use of revelation outside the Bible is pointless until the Bible, itself, can be used to demonstrate the need for the additional revelation. Therefore, we need to share in Christian love with the ones to whom we are witnessing that we do not accept any authority outside the Bible. We have to help them understand that the discussion must be limited to the Bible if we are going to be part of an open conversation. Simply put, we must challenge these religious individuals to find their position in the Bible. That request is fair because they claim to believe that the Bible is true in some fashion. Remember, we are talking to a member of a "Bible cult," not to someone who rejects the Bible as authoritative! The cult member may reject portions of it, but they still claim to accept it generally.

Again, we would be wise to remember at this point that these people of the cults and other "Bible" religions are human and are likely as nervous as we are. They do not have instant answers to all questions, and they will feel just as embarrassed as we would if made to look foolish. Perhaps the difference in their ability to respond with quick answers rests in the fact that cult members usually talk more often about what they believe than the average Christian, at least in areas where they are a minority and have to stand up for what they believe. Also, many cultists have a handbook or memorized procedure they have been taught to follow. This practice is especially true of the Mormons; so we will use them as an example of how to establish the Bible as the only authority in a conversation and do so in a way that is respectful.

When the doorbell rings and you open the door, you discover those two nice-looking, well-dressed young men (sometimes women) who have parked their economy car on the street in front of your house. (It is winter, and bicycles are not practical.) After using the procedure identifying truth as the focus of your conversation (as explained in the "opening comments" section of this chapter), you are now ready to start the main part of your discussion. The Mormon missionaries will probably begin to tell you a story. The story is about a young boy named Joseph Smith who, through his supposed vision of God and Jesus Christ, was to have restored the truth of God to the earth, truth that they believe had been lost. In other words, they believe Joseph Smith was a latter-day prophet and that, therefore, prophets exist today. (Do not expect Mormons to begin discussing some of their far-out beliefs right away.) The logical principle they follow is to help the person with whom they are talking make a decision to believe that Joseph Smith is a prophet of God; then everything else Joseph Smith taught has to be right. When the Mormon comes to the part about Joseph Smith's vision, the following paragraph is what, in essence, you might consider saying.

"Excuse me; may I share something with you that I believe will help us in discussing what the truth of God is? I believe very strongly that you have the right to accept Joseph Smith as a prophet of God and that you also have the right to believe that the *Book of Mormon* is Scripture. But I must be honest with you, and I think that you want me to be. Although you believe in Joseph Smith and the *Book of Mormon*, I do not. Now, I probably did not take you by surprise. After all, you are here to convince me that the *Book of Mormon* is true and that Joseph Smith is a prophet of God. I can understand and appreciate your desire to bring others into your beliefs. Because, however, I do not believe that Joseph Smith is a prophet or that the *Book of Mormon* is scripture (and I don't mean that statement to sound hateful, just honest), you could quote to me Joseph Smith and the *Book of Mormon,* and it would have no meaning. The only authority I accept is the Bible. If you hope to show me that your position is true, you must do so from the Bible."

Several things are happening at this point. First, you are not being unfair; you are being honest. You are asking the Mormon missionary to do with you what you would have to do with a Jewish individual who rejected the New Testament and accepted only the Old. You would have to limit your discussion with your Jewish friend to the Old Testament until such time as you demonstrated that the Old Testament points to the New. Only after he sees that the Old Testament teaches a need for the New will he logically be open to look at it.

Secondly, you have stopped the cult individual's normal presentation in a respectful way. Even if the person with whom you are talking tries to continue with his presentation, he will have to do so with this new understanding that using the Bible will be the only way he will be able to convince you of his position.

Thirdly, you have set before the Mormon a proposition encouraging him to study the Bible truly in an attempt to find what he believes in it. The first major step in leading a Mormon to the biblical Christ is getting him to study the Bible. This prerequisite is true of all "Bible" cult or religious individuals. What is his reaction to this restriction? I have yet to see a Mormon who will not take the challenge if properly presented. This acceptance does not mean that he will follow through with his promise. Human nature is still human nature. If he does seem hesitant to begin searching the Bible for his beliefs, ask him in a loving way why he is hesitant. If you are careful and polite, the Bible challenge approach sets the right direction for the conversation. I remember one occasion while I was talking with a Mormon missionary who referred to the *Pearl of Great Price* as Scripture. He stopped immediately, remembering that I did not accept the book as Scripture, and apologized! He, too, was being kind and respectful. Honesty and politeness go a long way toward creating the proper atmosphere.

Where will the conversation go from this point? We must understand that, in a friendly discussion with religious people, we can never follow an exact pattern. These conversations are very fluid in motion, and they quite easily take sudden, unexpected directions. What we must do to be prepared is to gather as many tools for teaching as possible. Our toolbox must include Bible verses, of course, but also reasonable logic that is consistent with Scripture. An example would be the questions listed below that a Christian could ask the cult individual at appropriate times during the conversation.

Question: *If you discovered that what you believe disagreed with the Bible, would you change what you believe?*

This important question causes the person (we are seeking to point to Christ) to evaluate his own willingness to follow his leadership blindly and at all costs. This question truly helps clarify the issues, but you may be shocked with the answers you receive. Some religious people are not willing to elevate their leaders' teachings above the Bible. (Again, remember that we are talking about people in a "Bible cult".) Unfortunately, many others from "Bible cults" will accept the writings of their leaders over the Bible. Generally, most of the religious individuals with whom you talk will refuse to accept the possibility of disagreement between the Bible and their leaders at all. The normal response from "Bible cult" followers tends to be that if the Bible seems to disagree with what they believe or their leadership teaches, it is simply a matter of researching and finding out what the Bible really is saying. Once that is done, then the disagreement with the Bible will be resolved in their favor. Sometimes, they are so certain that research will show them to be right that they feel no need to do it. However, they may do it for you so that they can convince you that you are wrong. We must see whatever reason causes a person to study the Bible as good. Many times, people who have researched the Bible to prove it wrong have come to the conclusion it is right because of their research. Our God is big enough to defend what He has written. This reliance on our sovereign God is the advantage in giving people time to think through and research issues. If we pressure them relentlessly before they have time to check out the issues, they may leave acknowledging what the Bible says but with the feeling that they have just been talking to a used car salesman! (For the record, I want everyone to know that I believe that honest used car salesmen are out there.)

Even though many of these cult individuals will respond favorably to respecting the Bible as an authority worth their response, you will, however, meet some that will strongly place their leadership and their revelations above the Bible. The following questions might be asked:

Question: *Where did your leader or leadership get authority?*

Possible cult response: from God.

Question: *Do you believe that the Bible teaches your leader has that authority?*

If the cult response is yes, then the logical question becomes: *Where does the Bible make such a statement?*

Ultimately, the following question becomes the final issue and is asked when it becomes increasingly clear that the person with whom one is talking is choosing his or her beliefs over the Bible.

Question: *Have you decided that your prophet (or leader or teachings or writings) is/are more trustworthy than the Bible?*

Everyone makes a decision about whom or what he trusts. For example, Mormons teach that Joseph Smith was a prophet of God and that other modern day prophets lead the Mormon Church. Mormons trust Joseph Smith and their prophets for truth. We trust the Bible. Here is the challenge we are putting before them. Are they so confident in what their leadership teaches and what they personally believe that, if they discovered the Bible truly taught something else, they would still choose their religious system over the Bible?

One very important thing to remember at this point is that you must not ever begin to think of these people as "pushovers." Many of them are proficient in presenting what they believe. Our task is not to convince them of our position, but to share in love the biblical Christ. God is not a "pushover" either, and when He is ready, He can change the heart of the most wicked or most religious individual, bringing that person to Himself.

In review: the purpose of establishing biblical authority with a cult organization that claims at least a partial belief in the Bible is twofold. Once again, we do not have to use the exact method used here, but we should attempt to present these two previously stated positions in the form of a loving challenge.

1. Does the Bible allow for the cult's claim to divine authority, such as Joseph Smith's claim to being a prophet? (This question does not involve attacking Joseph Smith or their belief's integrity. Instead, we are challenging them to discover if the Bible allows authority outside itself.)

    2. Is the cult individual able to present his/her position from the Bible alone?

Book of Mormon

One philosophy of evangelism today teaches that one way to witness to Mormons is to use the *Book of Mormon* references that contradict the Mormon position. Despite what Mormons might claim, the *Book of Mormon* does not teach Mormon doctrine as Mormons usually believe it today. It basically teaches traditional Bible doctrine with "baptismal regeneration" and "the Bible is not complete" thrown in. Perhaps without Joseph Smith's intentions, this similarity has turned into a profitable situation for the Mormon Church. When people begin exploring Mormonism, they usually read the *Book of Mormon* first. Potential converts walk away from this Mormon scripture easily convinced that Mormonism is not much different than traditional Christianity, except that Mormonism must have more of the truth than the rest of the Christian denominations!

So how did the *Book of Mormon* come to disagree with Mormonism in many ways? The answer may not be complicated at all. The fact is that the *Book of Mormon* was written in the early days of Mormonism before most of the extreme doctrines were developed. Because of this gap in time, Christians can actually use certain verses in the *Book of Mormon* to demonstrate that Mormonism does not agree with its own book, the *Book of Mormon*. (However, we should remember that the other writings of Mormonism more accurately reflect their doctrine.) Examples of *Book of Mormon* verses that disagree with Mormonism are: Alma 18:26-28, which teaches that God is Spirit; Mosiah 15:1-2, 5, which teaches that Jesus is God; and Moroni 8:18, which teaches that God does not change.

Some brilliant Bible scholars and cult researchers can capably demonstrate the inconsistency of Mormonism through the use of the *Book of Mormon.* I have great respect for these individuals and do not in any way wish to criticize their excellent research. Most of us, however, run into a problem with this approach. Once we choose to use the *Book of Mormon* as an authority, we give the Mormon with whom we are talking the right to use it also. By using it, we recognize its authority, and we can no longer say to the Mormon that the Bible must be the only authority in our discussion. Let's face it; in most conversations revolving around the *Book of Mormon*, a Mormon who is out sharing his beliefs will probably know better than most Christians how to use this book. Besides, if we do not believe it is Scripture, what it says really makes no difference in a search for truth.

Gary Vertican, a fellow Christian missionary in Utah, had a Mormon friend who asked him the following common questions. [4] The conversation went something like this:

Mormon: Do you have a *Book of Mormon?*
Gary: Yes, I received it as a gift.
Mormon: Well, are you reading it?

Gary:	Yes, I have been researching it. Let me ask you a question. Do you have a Bible?
Mormon:	Yes, and I believe in the Bible.
Gary:	Well, are you reading it?

This response on Gary's part was excellent. He shifted the issue back to the Bible. Normally the Mormon individual wants to center on the *Book of Mormon*. Even though researching the development of religious literature is a fascinating study, the truth is that we do not have to read the *Book of Mormon* or know its doctrines to witness to Mormon people. What is more important is our personal preparation in Bible study. The Spirit uses the Bible to give spiritual life, and without spiritual life, no one has the spiritual consciousness to understand spiritual truth.

New World Translation

Jehovah's Witnesses present a unique challenge in witnessing. They have rewritten the Bible in what they call *The New World Translation*. (The Reorganized Church of Jesus Christ of Latter-day Saints has done the same thing in their *Inspired Version of the Bible*.) The Jehovah's Witnesses claim that great Bible scholars were involved in the translation, but I am not aware of anyone who has seen a list that would allow examination of the translation scholars and their credentials (at least at the time of this writing).

What do we do when we meet someone who belongs to a cult that has rewritten the Bible? We should not overemphasize the difference between the translations until we encounter a clear disagreement. Nothing is wrong with being honest (when we see a discrepancy between our version and theirs) and sharing at that time that we do not accept their translation, as long as we do so with a loving attitude. As the conversation progresses, we would be wise to present Bible verses which teach the biblical way of salvation, keeping salvation as the focus. Interestingly, in some cases we will find that the verses we are using are almost the same in the cult version. Where our version and their version disagree, we need to attempt to demonstrate the true biblical position. Knowing Hebrew or Greek would certainly be advantageous, but as most people do not, the use of other good translations may prove helpful, if the individuals with whom we are talking are open-minded enough to do research of this sort. Comparing passages of Scripture where discrepancies between versions exist with passages that teach the same doctrine where disagreement does not exist, builds a foundation of truth. This process is often lengthy. Patience and loving concern for these religious but lost individuals are the keys.

Jewish and Islamic Religions

For the record, historically Islam and Judaism are categorized as religions and not labeled cults. Although these two religions are radically different in several major ways, they have aspects of similarities. Because Judaism, Islam, and Christianity have very close ties historically, Christians find many points of connection to begin witnessing. An example is Abraham, who is respected by all three belief-systems. Interestingly, witnessing to Muslim and Jewish people involves some of the same issues associated with the cults, but in reverse. The challenge is to be able to present a portion of the Bible (i.e. New Testament) to them despite the fact that they disagree with it either totally or partially. Even though both religions embrace aspects of the Bible, to begin looking at the New Testament concept of Christ will be a major jump. These people will have to see Christ in us first before they will look for Him in Scripture.

Most Jewish and Islamic mission programs discovered years ago that perhaps the most effective way to reach devoted religious people was through building relationships. The wisdom of finding common ground that both sides accept has been used to open doors for many years now. Initially avoiding the battle between conflicting doctrines, these Christian missionaries sought to become friends with the Jewish and Muslim people they desired to reach with the gospel. Learning how to appreciate culture without sacrificing truth provides acceptance and leads to opportunities to share Christ. Once the relationship is built, the common ground of the Old Testament can act as a firm foundation to reach into the New Testament.

Relationship building and cultural understanding are great strategies for reaching not only Jewish and Islamic people, but also all religions and cults. In Utah, living in a city that was ninety-five percent

Mormon, Beabea (my wife) and I would have had a simpler time of interacting with people by focusing on the major surface level of Mormonism, but doing so would have prevented the true formation of relationships. We found that the Mormon culture was everywhere we went; that presence, however, brought us as Christians into immediate disagreement and conflict. Instead, we looked for the sub-cultures of our society that would allow to us to work with people and build relationships. I joined local public school committees, helped in the pro-life program, and learned to hunt (a big sub-culture in Utah). Beabea gave horse-riding lessons and became involved in local equine organizations. We became part of the western culture. Once relationships developed into trust, we were able to bring in the Bible to share the message of salvation.

Non-Bible Cult

Other types of religious cults are in existence today, the origins for many of which began in Far Eastern religions and philosophies. Many of these ancient beliefs, however, have changed in the process of coming to the United States. They have westernized, often becoming part of the New Age movement and even taking on Christian terms to be more acceptable. Interaction with people from these kinds of backgrounds takes a variety of forms. The individual to whom we are witnessing may appear very American, with a high degree of intellectual sophistication, or he may look Asian, with a distinct politeness. He may be a Native American clothed in modern or ethnic dress, or he may come from some unknown background dressed in a robe, talking to us in an almost spaced-out condition, and leaving us wondering if he knows that we are there at all. The truth is that no absolute way exists of recognizing people who are involved in these religions. They come in all shapes, sizes, races, and cultures. This diversity should be a good reminder that the religion is not the issue, but, instead, the person in all his/her uniqueness with whom we desire to share Christ.

So, what do we do when we meet someone who believes that the Bible is only a good book or who does not accept it as an authority at all? First, we need to understand the fundamental difference between all other religion and biblical Christianity. We covered this point earlier, but we need to touch on it once more. A true believer in Christ has a relationship with the real God of the universe.

Outside of biblical Christianity, historic western (including European as well as American) religions and cults do not have the true God; so many seek to fill the void created by His absence with religious ritual. Keep in mind that these religious people are not biblically Christian, although they may call themselves such. The true believer has God; the western religious devotee has a void he is seeking to fill.

Now we come to the people who have embraced an eastern religion. The real God is absent here also, leaving a void in their lives. Many eastern religions, however, do not try to fill the void, but rather claim that it is desirable. They teach that the mind is free when it is empty. The searching restlessness that comes from missing God is healed through discipline. God is replaced with the mantra, a word or phrase repeated over and over to help empty the mind. Transcendental Meditation or TM is not meditation on what is truth but a deliberately sustained emptiness which gives spiritual forces ample opportunity to fill the void left by having no God in the person's life. In fact, the mantra is often thought to be the name of a supernatural being (possibly ancestor or alien from space) that may become an individual's spirit guide. To reach these people, we must first realize that no need for God exists within their beliefs. The Christian usually cannot share his message through the Bible to them. Instead, he must present the Bible through himself to the religious person he is trying to reach. We will talk a little more about that concept in a moment.

Because these people are not interested in the Bible, should we leave it out of our witnessing? Absolutely not! We must never apologize for believing the Bible to be the Word of God. To do so would be like a Roman soldier apologizing for bringing his sword with him in battle. We do, however, need to find a common ground upon which to approach the discussion as Paul did in his Mars Hill sermon found in Acts 17:22-31. Listen to his approach:

> *Ye men of Athens, I perceive that in all things ye are too superstitious. For as I passed by, and beheld your devotions, I found an altar with this inscription, TO THE UNKNOWN GOD. Whom therefore ye ignorantly worship, him declare I unto you.*

Point One: God is knowable!

God that made the world and all things therein, seeing that he is Lord of heaven and earth, dwelleth not in temples made with hands; Neither is worshipped with men's hands, as though he needed any thing, seeing he giveth to all life, and breath, and all things.

Point Two: God is self-sustained and not limited to objects in His existence!

And hath made of one blood all nations of men for to dwell on all the face of the earth, and hath determined the times before appointed, and the bounds of their habitation.

Point Three: God is in control!

That they should seek the Lord, if haply they might feel after him, and find him, though he be not far from every one of us: For in him we live, and move, and have our being; as certain also of your own poets have said, For we are also his offspring.

Point Four: God is personally interested in people's lives!

Forasmuch then as we are the offspring of God, we ought not to think that the Godhead is like unto gold, or silver, or stone, graven by art and man's device.

Point Five: God cannot be understood by human reasoning!

And the times of this ignorance God winked at; but now commandeth all men every where to repent: Because he hath appointed a day, in the which he will judge the world in righteousness by that man whom he hath ordained.

Point Six: God will judge wrong and will hold people personally accountable for their actions!

Whereof he hath given assurance unto all men, in that he hath raised him from the dead.

Point Seven: God has made provision for victory over the wrong for which people should be judged!

Paul was using scripturally-based logic. He shared with these people on Mars Hill that God is personal and knowable. We can derive three key concepts from this fact:

1. <u>God has spoken</u> (Hebrews 1:1-2). We can share with the religious individual that God has truly communicated with us in human language. The obvious question, even if not immediately recognized, is: "What did He say?" This question opens the door for us to use the Bible.
2. <u>God has come to us</u> (1 Timothy 3:16). The important message of biblical Christianity is the fact that God has done the work for us. He made the effort to reach man. This truth sets

biblical Christianity apart from the religious world, which is making every understood or guessed effort to reach God or some other high thing.

3. <u>Christ is God, and He is personal</u> (Titus 2:13). We need to take the same approach with these people that Philip did with the Ethiopian eunuch (Acts 8:35). We must present the person of Christ, introducing these people to the Savior, and we must share what He has done for us as well as for them and how they may receive His gift of eternal life.

In dealing with eastern religions, we need to realize that the God void in people's lives is probably the reason they joined the cult group that they did. This very real need allows us to emphasize the peace of God in our lives as well as other Christians' lives (Philippians 4:7). Knowing God is not just an emotional experience which gives the sensation of peace. Rather, knowing God brings satisfied, confident peace based on solid promises from God that He will keep His word and do the job of saving us if we put our trust in His Son.

Finally, in review, when talking with the individual that does not accept the Bible, whether he is from an eastern religion or simply a modern humanist, the believer will often find his approach necessarily different than in witnessing to someone who already believes that the Bible is God's Word. We see the depth of this difference in the fact that we may more readily deal with a religious individual who believes the Bible from the Bible. The believer shares the gospel message to the religious person through the Bible. With a religious person who rejects the Bible, however, the gospel message from the Bible must pass through the life of the believer in order to be shared with that individual. The Bible's credibility is established not in its claim to be God's Word, but through the evidence demonstrated by the actions of the one who believes it.

Finally, we must remember that, in any case, the consistent, biblical life of a believer is the necessary evidential support for the gospel message in all witnessing opportunities, whether the individual to whom we are speaking believes the Bible or not.

Three

Communicative Witnessing

What is communication? Such a simple question seems like it should have a simple answer. People all around the planet share words every single day. Is communication taking place? Or are words just being used without understanding? This chapter deals with the key to evangelistic efforts, not only with religious individuals but with all people everywhere. The reality is that, without communication, effective witnessing is not taking place. Christians may be sharing the gospel, but those they are trying to reach are not grasping it.

Learn by Listening

Again, we consider the question: what is communication? Is communication when I talk to another person? No, talking is just talking. Is communication when the other person hears me? No, hearing is just hearing. Then what is communication? Communication takes place when the thoughts as they existed in one person's mind form accurately in the mind of another because of or despite background, culture, religious understanding, and/or previous interaction. Communication can then be defined as the act of capturing intact the thoughts of another person and transferring intact your thoughts to another person. This definition doesn't mean that you or the other individual involved are in agreement. It does mean that you clearly understand what the other person is thinking and that he or she understands what you are thinking as you interact with each other.

This task of communication is not easy. It requires one to take into account the above mentioned background, culture, religious understanding, and previous interaction involving the person with whom one seeks to communicate; then, one must choose words carefully based on language that will transfer one's thoughts to the other person accurately. To do so requires an ability that most people do not use often, and those that do use it do not use it often enough! The ability to which I am referring is listening. Listening is a tremendous skill that, if practiced properly and regularly, will allow us to discover accurately what is happening in the minds of others. Listening with the attempt to capture another's thoughts is the closest thing to mind reading most of us will ever achieve, and it works! I am not talking about letting someone talk to us while we sit and think about other things, putting our time in so that we can say we are listening. Instead, we should remain quiet, concentrating on what the speaker is sharing with us and why, and speaking only to receive clarification of a statement that is not clear. We can do so by asking questions and then listening to the responses. Also, I do not mean being a robot and not relaxing while you communicate. What I mean is talking less and listening more!

Unfortunately, many witnessing opportunities are not effective because Christians do not practice listening. Instead, Christians practice talking a lot, and they walk away from such opportunities convinced that they shared Christ with another. The truth is that, although they have shared Christ, they have not communicated Him. True listening allows us to understand another person so that, when we begin to share the gospel, we will know how to share so that the person with whom we are talking will correctly grasp the concepts that we want him to hear.

One of the keys to listening is being polite. We need to develop our manners and not always be concerned about getting the last word. Remember, God does not do all His work in one conversation. We must learn to trust God and politely share, as He allows, even if we do not get everything said that we want to say.

I am about to repeat myself in a slightly different way, seeking to improve on my communication to you, the reader! Communication is the most important factor in reaching the people of the cults and religions of the world with the biblical Christ. If you do not truly communicate what you want to say, you are wasting your time talking. This point is very important: unless communication takes place, no actual witnessing has taken place! Whew! Talk about overkill! I am fairly certain by now that I have communicated to you how important this point is, or at least that I believe it is important. In fact, from my point of view, if you do not believe that effort in communication is important, you might as well put this book down and go watch TV, an activity which will require very little effort and allow an electronic, non-human object to communicate intensely to your mind. Remember, serving God is hard work that will require self-discipline. Are you ready to listen and learn?

Define Terms

Defining terms is a crucial part of communication. I have shared Christ with cult individuals and have had them say, "I've talked with a lot of Christians before, but you're the first one who has been able to explain to me what you believe." This failure to explain well does not mean that these Christians did not know what they believed or the biblical reasons for believing it. It does mean that they had great difficulty in expressing their beliefs so that the cult person could understand what was being shared. My ability to explain also does not mean that I am smart. It does mean that I listened! Think of a time perhaps when you may have been in a witnessing situation with a religious individual who did not believe in biblical salvation, and although the person with whom you were speaking agreed with everything you said, you knew that his beliefs were not the same as yours!

Let us examine the actions of some Mormon people for a moment, using them as an example. We desire to do so respectfully but honestly. Mormonism is very much an "end justifies the means" religion. This statement sounds harsh, but I do not make it with any malice. I make it based on the many conversations I have had with Mormons. In most cases, the Mormon individual is not making a direct attempt at deception but is, instead, simply choosing to withhold some of the facts about Mormonism until the one he is seeking to convert has made his or her commitment to the Mormon belief that Joseph Smith was a prophet of God. Once a person accepts Joseph Smith as a prophet and, logically, the leadership of the Mormons as prophets, then whatever they are teaching must be right, because they are receiving revelation from God! Even the strangest doctrine imaginable takes on credibility when it is linked with God.

One area in which Mormon evangelists quite commonly use deception (purposeful or not) is in the unique Mormon belief about the Godhead. Mormons believe in what they call exaltation. This belief is that God was once a man (probably the savior) of a previous earth. He did what he was supposed to do and, as a reward, earned the right to become the ruling god of this earth where we live. Further, most probably God's god was a man on an earth that existed previous to God's home planet, who did what he was supposed to do and became the ruling god of the earth where our God grew up. Each man on our earth also has the opportunity of going on and ruling his own earth if he is obedient to the Mormon gospel. In fact, the basic belief is that the whole universe is filled with gods producing men who become gods who produce men. This process goes on from eternity past to eternity future. Mormons have a saying: "As man is, God once was. As God is, man may become." Joseph Smith stated, "You have got to learn how to be gods yourselves."[5]

Although the informed Mormon believes these facts, if they were presented to him, he might reply, "That belief is not Mormon doctrine." But if he were asked if these things were true Mormon concepts, his honest reply, if he were pressed for an answer, might be yes. You may be asking yourself how he could honestly answer both ways. The answer is simple in the Mormon's mind. For some Mormons, Mormon doctrine is that which appears in the standard works, that is, *Book of Mormon, Doctrine and Covenants, Pearl of Great Price,* and the Bible ("as far as it is translated correctly"). Any other concepts held by the Mormon Church are not official doctrines, although most Mormons believe them and are convinced that they are true. Mormons come to this conclusion despite the fact that these other concepts appear as doctrine in Bruce McConkie's book, *Mormon Doctrine.* In dealing with Mormons, we may well find ourselves defining the term "doctrine" – what the word actually means and what they believe it means. Furthermore, do they use other words that describe what they believe, such as "concept"? Are concepts just as important as doctrine?

Are we making a mountain out of a molehill by placing so much emphasis on defining terms? I challenge you to try to communicate effectively without defining terms such as these. You will find yourself running in circles going nowhere if you ignore this issue!

In all fairness, some Mormons do not hide behind this line of reasoning, but openly admit this idea of "gods producing men who become gods" as doctrine. Others will usually admit that the standard works teach the plurality of gods, but these ideas are mysteries with which we do not need to concern ourselves. You will hear as many explanations of this concept as there are Mormons. For this reason, when witnessing to cult people, approaching each one individually without a preconceived idea of what he believes is so important. For this reason, we need to listen to the terms he uses and learn to adjust the terms we use, not changing our doctrine to match error but changing our words to clarify what is truth. The reason we took so much space on this point is to help you, the reader, to be intensely aware of the importance of defining what you believe and not taking what you hear at surface value. We must remember that the cults as well as other more accepted religions often use the same terms we use, but they have redefined those terms in their systems of theology. We will illustrate this point by giving a testimony as a Mormon could legitimately do. Even though we are once again using Mormonism as an example, other cult followers could make these kinds of statements based on their theological definitions of these words.

Possible Mormon testimony: *"I believe that Jesus the Christ is the very Son of God. I have received His teachings, and I believe Jesus Christ is my Savior. I have faith in Christ, and I believe in Him. Because of His death and sacrifice, I have been saved by God's grace. I know I am going to heaven when I die. I made the decision, and I have been born again. I am a child of God."*

What you have just read probably sounded like basic Bible doctrine. Most people coming for membership in a local church would be quite welcome with the testimony just given. Should we wonder at all then that often Christians who have talked to Mormons and other cult individuals come away concluding that they are fellow believers? True, not every Mormon will be this "deceptive" in what he believes, but some are quite proficient at verbal camouflage. They have learned to adjust their definitions to match the words of the person with whom they are talking.

We must also remember that this terminology problem is not necessarily a deliberate deception. It stems, as we have already mentioned, from the fact that the cults have taken biblical terms and given them new definitions. Cult members can say these terms without intentionally lying. None of the above Mormon testimony contained actual lies. If I were a Mormon defining the terms used as a Mormon would define them, I could have honestly said the above words without lying. Expressing the testimony shared above, however, would have been a deliberate avoidance of terminology that might trigger a reaction in the non-Mormon I was trying to convert. The logical goal of a Mormon in such a situation is to use appropriate terms that help convince the people with whom he is talking that Mormonism really is not much different from what they believe. His point is that Mormons are Christian, but in fact, Mormons believe that they are actually more Christian than other "Christian" denominations because they have more truth than other "Christian" denominations!

Now, let us get back to that Mormon testimony. If he did not lie, then what did he really mean when he said the words?

Explanation of Mormon testimony:

I believe that Jesus the Christ is the very Son of God: Mormonism teaches that Jesus Christ is a literal-born son of Father God and Mother God in the pre-existence before coming to earth. They also teach that all humans here on earth were born in the same way in this pre-existence before coming to our planet.

I have received His teachings: This statement means that the Mormon has embraced the Mormon Church and its doctrine. To receive Christ is often understood to mean receiving the Church of Jesus Christ of Latter-day Saints, thus becoming a Mormon.

I believe Jesus Christ is my Savior: Mormons teach that Jesus is the helper. His death provides opportunity for the Mormon to earn all the rewards God has for Him. Jesus' death has merit, but the Mormon must earn that merit. He must merit the merit of Christ. Mormons do their best, and then Jesus does the rest (if the heart is right and the motives are pure and the desire is sincere, etc., etc., etc.).

I have faith in Christ, and I believe in Him: To believe or have faith is the first step in a long series of steps that are necessary if one hopes to be with God some day. Faith is also thought of in another way. When a Mormon says he has faith, he can mean that he has the right faith. In other words, he is of the Mormon faith.

Because of His death and sacrifice, I have been saved by God's grace: God's grace comes as a result of Christ's death, but it provides only resurrection, as it also does for everyone, including non-Mormons. What you get beyond resurrection is called exaltation, and you must earn that privilege. Everyone on the entire earth will be saved by God's grace, but that salvation does not mean, according to the Mormon, that everyone will be with God. Again, the salvation of which he is speaking is the resurrection of mankind. Everyone will be resurrected, but not everyone will be with God. The Mormon must earn that honor.

I know I am going to heaven when I die: The Mormon knows he is going to heaven. Mormons believe in three kingdoms or heavens, but God only dwells in the highest heaven. Everybody on earth is going to one of these kingdoms (with maybe a few minor exceptions.) How worthy one is in this life determines where one goes. Therefore, a Mormon knows that he will be in heaven when he dies; he just does not know which one.

I made the decision, and I have been born again: Being born again means baptism to most Mormons. They come to this conclusion by misinterpreting John 3:5. We will deal with that misunderstood passage in a later chapter.

I am a child of God: Everyone is a child of God according to Mormon doctrine. Remember, all people who have ever lived were born in a pre-existence to Father God and Mother God (or Mother Gods).

Even reading this short explanation of Mormon terms can lead to a negative attitude toward Mormon people. The natural reaction (how can anyone be so stupid as to believe such concepts?) is unfair. Intellectual people worldwide look at biblical Christianity and wonder how we could be so stupid as to believe in a virgin birth, a six-day creation, a worldwide flood, and a resurrected God-man. The reason the Mormon Church is wrong or any other religion is wrong is not because their beliefs appear strange, but because their beliefs disagree with the Bible. We dare not forget this important fact.

When we talk with people from the cults, we must be in the practice of defining our terms throughout the entire conversation. As I wrote earlier, the biggest problem I find with some tracts is the careless way their writers use biblical terms, expecting everyone to know what they mean. This mistake easily occurs in a witnessing conversation, also. We must not take for granted that the people with whom we are talking understand what we are saying. Often they do not, and until they do, nothing can be accomplished. Have I said those words before? This process of establishing communication can sometimes take hours. I have seldom talked with a cult individual for less than an hour unless time constraints forced otherwise.

I remember an incident that took place at the Bible college I attended. A couple of fellows with heads shaved bald who were wearing white robes and sandals walked on campus wanting something to eat and drink. Some of the students assisted them in this need. As they were leaving, another student and I asked if we could talk to them. They told us that they had an eternity of time (or something to that effect). We all four sat down on the grass, each of us looking for ants. (In Florida, one does not sit down on the grass without looking for ants.) We were not very far along in the conversation before we realized why they did not want to sit on the ants. They did not fear being bitten. Instead, they believed that the ants were their brothers, and they did not want to harm them. At this point in the conversation, for us to remember that these people were wrong not because of a strange belief but because they disagreed with the Bible was very important.

The conversation seemed to go on for hours (probably not that long) without the feeling of accomplishing anything. The men in robes would share with me doctrine totally contrary to everything I understood the Bible to teach, but when I shared in return the truths of God's Word, they would nod their heads in agreement. I was at the point of screaming inside, and several times I came very close to giving up. Nevertheless, they were quite willing to continue the conversation; so we remained. The opportunity seemed as if it took forever to arise, but finally I expressed a certain biblical truth in a carefully worded phrase based on listening to their explanations of what they believed. For the first time since we started, they admitted that they did not believe what I said. Real communication still took awhile, but that point was the breakthrough. Ultimately, we were able to share Christ with them so that, for the first time in their lives, they understood who He really is and His way to God. They decided to leave. Time in the universe ran out or something.

When we witness to these people, we must realize that we will normally not reach them in a ten-minute visit. We must be willing to give of our time, hours of our lives if necessary, to share Christ with these dear people. We may find ourselves growing weary in well doing. Because of this terminology problem and the limits of any one human mind, to be totally prepared in knowing every doctrine of every cult and what the perfect response is at any given moment is impossible. Therefore, many Christians are afraid to witness to religious individuals, especially those from the cults. We cannot carry this burden when we witness to these people. We must remember that the Holy Spirit is the One who will lead them to Christ. We should be as ready as possible, though, and that readiness requires determination on our part.

Know the Meaning of Biblical Terms

In order to define terms for others, we must know the biblical definitions of those terms ourselves. Secondly, we must know the Bible reasons and references for those definitions the Bible supports. Ask yourself this question: do I believe what I believe about God because I have found it in the Bible, or do I believe what I believe because my pastor has said that these doctrines are in the Bible?

Our pastors are wonderful people, but their authority ends the second they teach something that is contrary to God's Word. We should not depend on any one person to baby-sit our understanding of God's truth. We must respect our pastors and their years of learning and study, but we should never substitute that respect for our own learning and study. I was a missionary-pastor for years, and I know that most pastors would agree one hundred percent with the statement I just made. We should know what we believe biblically, but we should also know the Bible reason why we believe it. First, we must learn where Scripture teaches a doctrine, and secondly, we must learn what these biblical terms that we use all the time really mean. I challenge you to take time to sit down and write out biblical definitions and their Scripture references for the terms you use. The appendix in this book is designed to help you do that kind of research. For now, we will take a moment to look at some biblical terms we all use on a regular basis.

Saved

Let us examine this very familiar biblical word that we often use without very much thought. The dictionary definition of "saved" is to be delivered from danger or peril. A biblical definition of saved might be to be delivered from God's wrath through a personal trust in Christ (Romans 5:9; John 3:36; 1 Thessalonians 1:10). In this definition, we would probably need to define the term "wrath." What is the wrath of God? The answer is the biblical hell (Revelation 14:10). To be saved might simply be defined: "I am saved from hell and going to heaven when I die." Now, however, defining the terms of "heaven" and "hell" that I used so easily may become necessary. Do you understand the importance of what I am sharing with you? I dare not take any word that I use for granted, because the person with whom I am talking may define it differently than I do.

There certainly is more to the biblical fact of salvation than has just been listed, but what we shared would be a good start in understanding the word "saved".

As a side note, another common term in the United States is "commitment." This term is not so much biblical as a current cultural term that has enjoyed wide acceptance even overseas. Because it is not so much a biblical term as a descriptive word, we will encounter some real challenges in using it with religious people. The word "commitment" may to the cult individual's mind actually seem to support the idea that salvation is by works. He may see commitment as implying that we have something to contribute in the salvation process.

Another term used overseas (especially in former communist countries in Eastern Europe) is the word "repented." Believers there will sometimes express themselves when describing their salvation experience as "I repented" instead of "I was saved." Salvation cost something under communism, and those believers correctly viewed repentance as a serious part of the salvation process. The word "repent" anchors itself in Scripture very well, but it will still need to be defined so that religious people will understand its usage and not see it as action of merit, part of a works salvation.

Receiving Christ

This term, of course, is very common in Christian circles. Most important is the fact that it is a very biblical term. John 1:12 defines "receiving" as believing. Using Scripture to define the terms we use is very powerful. What, however, is "believing"? The verse says that receiving Christ means that we believe on the name of Jesus Christ in order to become a child of God. So believing is receiving Christ. We accept Christ, and we become children of

God. Christ promises to do something for us, and we act upon His promise. Trust is a good definition of believing, but what is "trust"? Trust is not an emotion but a true reliance on another to do what is expected. When we trust Christ, we take the chance and run the risk that He will keep His promise of making us children of God. The Greek is literally to believe or trust "into" Christ.

Eternal Life

What about "eternal life"? We Christians like that phrase. Defining "eternal life" may not be so simple, though. Common responses might be "never dying" or "living forever." People who go to hell never cease to exist, and they certainly seem to "live" forever, although their existence is terrible. Again, using Scripture becomes the key. John 17:3 teaches that "this is life eternal, that they might know thee the only true God, and Jesus Christ, whom thou hast sent." Scripture defines eternal life as knowing the true God and His Son, Jesus Christ. Eternal life describes this wonderful, permanent relationship with God.

Here we go again. Knowing what we believe or why we believe it is not enough; we have to know how to communicate it. We must be able to share the meaning of biblical words with others. Before we can do so, we must learn to listen and ask for definitions. While we are concentrating on these key areas, we also have to stay alert to the fact that cult individuals will often adapt their terminology to match the terms of the person with whom they are talking.

Listening first to what other individuals believe will allow them to share definitions early in the conversation and help prevent them from adjusting explanations later to fit our doctrinal terms.

Use Terms That Communicate

Not only do we need to define terms, but we also need to use only those biblical expressions that will clarify what we are trying to say to the cult members. Often we discover these expressions by trial and error, learning during an actual conversation what works best for a particular person. A couple of examples here can illustrate what I mean. For instance, in witnessing to a Mormon, saying that "I know I will be in heaven when I die" would probably not be wise. As we demonstrated earlier, a Mormon believes that he will be in a heaven someday, for he may go to one of three possible heavens based on his works. According to Mormon theology, God only lives in the highest heaven. Therefore, a Mormon knows he will be in a heaven someday; he just does not know which one or that he will for certain be with God in the highest one. (Some Mormons may claim to know that they will be with God because they have been good enough.) Understanding these Mormon concepts, we need to share with our Mormon friends that we know we will be with God the Father when we die, not just in heaven. We may even discover that we need to clarify our wording even further. We may choose to use this phrase: I know that I will be with God the Father in heaven some day, getting His very best. I know that I will be with Him not because

I am good enough but because of my relationship to Jesus Christ. The Scripture verse backing this position is John 14:6.

If we are sharing Christ with a Jehovah's Witness, we may get his attention quickly by saying that we know we will be with Jehovah when we die. He does not really believe he has much chance for that honor, as his doctrine teaches that the one hundred forty-four thousand who get to be with Jehovah have already been selected. Inclusion in that number is, however, the highest possible reward a Jehovah's Witness can earn, while biblical Christians receive the presence of Jehovah through Christ apart from our works. Again, the Scripture verse backing this position is John 14:6.

When witnessing to any member of a cult or religion, we would also be wise not just to say carelessly, "The Scriptures teach this truth" (in reference to a certain position one holds). Remember, religions and cults have many scriptures. Instead, one would do well to say, "This truth is what God's Word, the Bible, teaches." This statement clarifies that the Scripture to which you are referring is the Bible, not some other book or writing.

Four

Priority Goal

In World War II, both sides used torpedo attack aircraft to destroy enemy warships. As the planes zeroed in on their intended objectives, anti-aircraft fire would come at them from a multitude of directions. During these intense moments, a pilot had to remember just one order from his training: stay on target!

Referring to Jesus Christ, Acts 4:12 states, "Neither is there salvation in any other: for there is none other name under heaven given among men, whereby we must be saved." The main direction and priority goal of all conversations with people is to see them come to a personal relationship with Christ, resulting in their salvation. Plenty of side issues will tempt us to talk about other things. Stay on target!

Focus on Salvation

We should have no question in our minds that the most important topic of all the topics available to discuss during a witnessing conversation is the subject of salvation. Ultimately, nothing else really matters. The proper awareness of God's true salvation is crucial to where we and anyone else will spend eternity.

When dealing with cults and their endless collection of peripheral issues (such as the Jehovah's Witnesses' position that the Bible commands their members to refuse blood transfusions), we have to make a decided effort to stay focused on their eternal destiny. We must zero in on salvation. For instance, if a Mormon comes to our door, we ought to avoid a discussion on polygamy if at all possible. The Mormon Church officially condemns the practice of polygamy today, but some Mormons in Utah still practice it, having two or more living wives. Usually, polygamists are excommunicated from the Mormon Church. Those Mormon members who do not become involved in actual polygamy may still believe in it from a theological and historical view. Mormon doctrine teaches that if a man's wife, who has been sealed in the temple to him for eternity, dies, and he is sealed to another wife, then he will be married to both in eternity. This concept is theological polygamy.

Proving that polygamy is wrong is not difficult, for 1 Timothy 3:2, 12 and Titus 1:6 teach the one-wife principle. Conceivably, you could prove to a Mormon that polygamy is wrong and have him leave your house still lost and facing eternity without the biblical Christ. We must get our priorities straight.

Three very important areas are worth discussing under the topic of salvation. All three of these topics fall naturally into place after the establishment of the Bible as your authority. These three key areas are:

1. The person of the Savior
2. The work of the Savior
3. The grace of God

The Person of the Savior

Showing someone Jesus is always worth taking whatever time it requires. Showing someone who Jesus is involves the very important fact that Jesus is God (Hebrews 1:8). Many people fail to grasp this great necessity to our salvation. If Jesus is not God (who by nature is an infinite being), then paying the eternal punishment for sin in a set period of time would have been impossible for Him. Only an infinite being such as God could suffer an eternal hell in a limited time span on the cross. Angels are holy beings without sin, but they are not infinite. As a limited being, one angel could not experience an eternity of hell for everyone. Justice would demand that one angel be placed in hell for each human that is to be saved, and all those angels would have to stay in hell forever to satisfy God's eternal holiness. If Jesus were an angel, even if He were the highest and best angel, He would not have been capable of redeeming mankind. Because most cults doctrinally lower Christ to the level of an angel or claim that He is only an angel, they must logically believe that He is not capable of saving them completely. And most cults do come to this conclusion. But how can they trust Christ for salvation if He is not capable of doing the job? If a cult individual, however, comes to the understanding that Jesus is really God, then this person will have the basis for trust in a powerful Savior who can truly save.

The Work of the Savior

Showing what Christ accomplished on the cross is also worth taking the time required. The wonderful truth is that Jesus has paid for personal sins and accomplished a lot more than just a general atonement that gives mankind the opportunity to prove themselves (1 John 2:1-2). John 3:14-16 and Romans 5:6-10 teach that Christ shed His blood to satisfy God's righteous anger toward sin. Hebrews 9:22 teaches that blood must be shed before sins can be forgiven, and Hebrews 10:10-14 teaches that Christ suffered only one time for our sins. (This position differs from the Roman Catholic view that He suffers over and over during Holy Communion.) Finally, Romans 3:24-25 teaches that faith in Christ's shed blood appropriates God's forgiveness of our sins (Acts 10:43), nothing else! This truth is what God says, despite the claim by a Mormon author that a personal belief in Christ's shed blood for salvation is just some Christians' opinion. (See *What the Mormons Think of Christ*, p. 31, first paragraph under "The blood of Christ" section. This Mormon publication is given away free at any Mormon visitor's center. You may, however, have to locate an old version to find the quote!) [6]

The Grace of God

Think of the excitement that would spread through true Christianity if we all grasped a true realization of the uniqueness of God's salvation and His amazing grace. Now, think of the spiritual thrill we get to experience when a member of a false religion or a cult understands this great truth for the first time. Just as Pilgrim placed at the foot of the cross the heavy load of sin that he bore on his back, religious people and cult members can place the weight and guilt of religious failure into the open hands of Christ and become free from the overwhelming burden of trying to be good enough to be accepted by God through their organizations. In a world of religion where people are trying to work their way to God, we bring the wonderful news that God has worked His way to man in the person of Christ. The struggle to be right with God is over when we trust Christ, by God's "undeserved favor" (the definition of grace), to make us right with God.

What Actually Saves Us

The cults often use a trap to confuse many Christians as to what actually saves them. What does save us? Does our believing save us? If I stop believing, am I still saved? One day, you may find yourself in the following situation with a cult member. You have just shared with him the fact that you do nothing for your salvation; Jesus has done it all. He smiles and makes this reply, "Oh, yes, you do. You have to ask Jesus to save you. We believe that we have to do so also, but we do not stop there. We add to that act many other things. We have no differ-ence between us, though. You do one work: believe. We do that work and more. You do one work; we do many. But we are both working for our salvation."

This kind of thinking is quite logical if you fall into the trap that believing is a work. This concept is dangerous, for it is quite anti-biblical. Think this idea through. When you trusted in Christ, did that trust earn the merit of Christ in your salvation? Did God give you so many points in heaven for trusting in His Son? No! Remember, one of the certain signs of a false religion is that a person must do something to earn the merit of Christ. Does our trusting save us? Again, the answer is no! Christ alone saves us. Trusting is merely the channel through which that saving power of Christ comes.

Let me illustrate. If my hands were dirty and I went to a sink to wash them, I would turn on the water faucet. Observe that turning on the water faucet is not what cleanses my hands; the water cleanses my hands. Turning on the water faucet merely creates the scenario that allows the water to clean my hands. So, too, our trusting in Christ is the scenario for Him to save us. One individual might have great trusting ability, while another might have little trusting ability. Christ can save both equally because their salvation does not depend on how much trust they have but on whom they trust!

Some groups today are making a major doctrinal mistake; they believe that their trusting saves them. They trust in their trust. With that logic, they have an "on again, off again" salvation; that is, they believe that they can lose their salvation when they stop trusting. Today they are trusting; tomorrow they may not be. The biblical fact is that Christ saves; therefore, we can never lose our salvation. Let us not make the mistake of trusting in our trusting. Let us do things the biblical way. Let us trust in Christ alone to save us.

Someone reading this may be thinking about John 6:28-29, which reads, *"Then said they unto him, What shall we do, that we might work the works of God? Jesus answered and said unto them, This is the work of God, that ye believe on him whom he hath sent."* Is Jesus teaching that believing is a work? Absolutely not: in fact, He teaches just the opposite. The important point to note is Jesus' reply. He stated that believing was the work of God, not a work of man!

Let us review this sensitive yet crucial subject. Trust (faith) is a necessary part of salvation but not the means of it. Salvation is by grace through the channel of faith (Ephesians 2:8-9). Prayer does not save. (Prayer that occurs in the salvation process is a verbal or mental acknowledgement of Jesus as the One who saves.) Our trust does not earn merit before God. We must not trust in the fact that we have trusted in Christ. We must trust Christ. Again, trust is the channel of salvation, not the means of it. The questions we need to ask ourselves are:

> Do I trust in my trust and its ability to save?
> Do I trust in a prayer I prayed to be saved?
> OR
> Do I truly trust in Christ alone to save me?

The day I truly understood this issue was a great day of deliverance in understanding my relationship with God. To comprehend that salvation truly is the work of God apart from my insignificant efforts caused me to realize that even my response to God as He drew me to Himself could not be a source of personal pride. Jesus paid it all; all to Him I owe!

To Believe or Not to Believe

We now come to another very important area regarding biblical salvation. We must understand the subtle difference between casual believing and truly trusting. I want to share a story with you that I have heard preachers use in sermons for many years. This illustration applies both to salvation and to the daily life of a Christian. In the year 1859, a famous tightrope walker, Charles Blondin, announced that he was going to put a tightrope across Niagara Falls and walk across it several times. Huge crowds of people showed up, and the story goes that Blondin actually performed this feat several times. Finally, he took a wheelbarrow and walked across the falls and back. Several versions exist of what happened next. According to one story, a person in the crowd grew so excited that he jumped up and said to the tightrope walker as the entertainer was just returning from his last stroll on the rope, "I believe that you are the best tightrope walker in the world; I believe that you could walk back and forth with that wheelbarrow a thousand times and never fall."

Charles Blondin replied, "Do you really believe that?"

The excited observer responded, "Yes, I believe that with all my heart!"

"Really?"

"Oh, absolutely!"

Blondin smiled and said, "Then get in the wheelbarrow."

The observer remained an observer. [7]

When it comes to salvation, believing that Jesus can save us is not enough. We must trust Him to do so. We must be willing to take the chance, run the risk, and trust that Christ will do what He promised to do, that He will do the job of taking us all the way into the presence of God in heaven successfully. We do not keep ourselves safe in salvation; Christ does! Getting us safely across the chasm that separates us from God is up to Him. Interestingly enough, that relationship is true of the Christian life also. Believing that God will take care of us is not enough. We must trust Him to do so.

Closing Comments

How one closes a conversation with religious people or cultists is just as important as how one opens it. A time usually comes in each discussion when those involved can sense that it is drawing to a close for any number of reasons. Perhaps a lot of areas have been discussed, and everyone needs time to think through the issues. Maybe a tension is developing that could be defused by a little time apart. Whatever the reason we sense the conversation should end, nothing is wrong in allowing this break to happen, even if we have not had the opportunity to present everything we wanted. We must believe that the Holy Spirit is working. Of course, God always works this way: on His schedule, not ours. The more we witness, the more we will become convinced that God's timing is much better than ours. It always has been.

We can sense some clues to know that a conversation is closing. The more one deals with a particular cult, the more one can identify what is happening. I will give an example. In the case of Mormons, an indication that the conversation may be drawing to a close is when they turn in the *Book of Mormon* and read a passage that is very important to them. Even if only the Bible has been used as an authority during the conversation up to this point, due to accepting the challenge given them to find what they believe in just the Bible (described in the chapter "Friendly Discussions" earlier in this book), most Mormons will not hesitate to use this *Book of Mormon* verse. The passage, Moroni 10:4, reads, "And when ye shall receive these things, I would exhort you that ye would ask God, the Eternal Father, in the name of Christ, if these things are not true; and if ye shall ask with a sincere heart, with real intent, having faith in Christ, he will manifest the truth of it unto you, by the power of the Holy Ghost."

Once he reads the verse, the Mormon will possibly say something to this effect: "I would like to share my testimony with you. I have done as this verse says and asked God if these things were true. He has shown me that they are true. I know that Joseph Smith was a prophet of God called to minister on the earth in these latter days. I know that the *Book of Mormon* is true scripture, just like the Bible, and I know that you can know so as well if you sincerely ask God. He will show you the truth through the power of the Holy Ghost."

Sounds impressive, does it not? Many people are brought into the Mormon Church because of this *Book of Mormon* challenge. Is it a valid request? Consider these issues.

1. Examine Moroni 10:4, and think through the logic behind it. What the passage is really saying is this: if you will ask God if these things are true, believing that they are true, He'll show you that they are true. In other words, if you make up your mind before you ask, then God will show you. An ancient philosopher once said, "We believe whatever we want to believe." [8] If I want to believe something sincerely enough, I will discover a reason to believe it.

2. I took this challenge before I understood the issues, when I first started studying Mormonism. What happened? Well, God showed me that Mormonism was not true, but He showed me through a study of the Bible in relationship to Mormonism.

3. I can make just as strong a claim through the testimony of the Holy Spirit in my life; I know I'm right. We must, however, have more than just an emotional impression that we are right. What if that emotional impression was due to

a hormone imbalance? The Bible must be the anchor to which we tie truth in a floating sea of religious emotion and confusion.

We do not belittle or question the working of the Holy Spirit in our lives today. We believe that the Holy Spirit is bearing witness with our spirit (Romans 8:16), that He is teaching born-again Christians (1 John 2:27), and that we cannot know God without Him (1 Corinthians 2:14). Nevertheless, we must have a consistent authority outside our personal experience to instruct us in what is right. The reason for this need should be obvious, and it is well illustrated with this excellent example given to me by Lloyd Larkin, a missionary for many years in Utah (world headquarters of the Mormons).

Let us pretend to take ten people of ten different religious belief systems and line them up, among them a Mormon, Jehovah's Witness, Christian Scientist, Roman Catholic; you can throw in a Baptist if you like. We instruct them to get down on their knees and spend a couple of minutes asking God what the true church is. One... two... three: down on their knees they go. They start praying. Time is up. They stand. We begin to inquire about the results of their prayers.

"Mr. Mormon, what organization did God show you is the true church?"

"Why, God told me that my church is the true church."

"Mr. Jehovah's Witness?"

"God showed me that my organization is the only one Jehovah recognizes on earth."

"Mr. Christian Scientist?"

"God showed me that our teachings are the only way to understand existence."

And on down the line you go, getting basically the same results. [9] We must have an authority outside ourselves to determine who is right, or we will have no way of knowing for certain. The Bible is that authority!

Passage to Remember

My experience has taught me about a passage of Scripture that is very effective in almost any witnessing situation, whether religious people are involved or not. This passage is simultaneously a great opening Scripture to reference, an excellent platform for a short conversation, and a good closing passage for all cults. The reference is 1 John 5:9-13. After the Mormon has shared Moroni 10:4 and his testimony, one of the best Bible references to use is the 1 John passage, because it deals with personal testimony, authority, and knowing truth. If possible, we must, when talking with anyone, leave him with something to think about until we have a chance to interact with him again. Let us examine together 1 John 5:9-13.

Verse 9 – *"If we receive the witness of men, the witness of God is greater: for this is the witness of God which He hath testified of His Son."* It is more important to have the personal testimony of God concerning Jesus than the opinion of any man.

Verse 10 – *"He that believeth on the Son of God hath the witness in himself."* We do not deny the testimony of the Holy Spirit in our lives, but as we are about to see, God's recorded Word is the more certain knowledge. *"He that believeth not God hath made Him a liar; because he believeth not the record that God gave of His Son."* What is God's true record?

Verses 11 and 12 – *"And this is the record, that God hath given to us eternal life, and this life is in His Son. He that hath the Son hath life; and he that hath not the Son of God hath not life."* The truth is simply stated. Works are completely removed. Based on the next verse, we know that the "life" spoken of here contextually is "eternal life." If you have Jesus, you have life, eternal life. If you do not have Jesus, you do not have life, eternal life. If you have Jesus, you have salvation. If you do not have Jesus, you do not have salvation. There is no in-between.

Verse 13 – *"These things have I written unto you that believe on the name of the Son of God; that ye may know that ye have eternal life, and that ye may believe on the name of the Son of God."* Remember from the previous chapter that terminology and definitions are crucial in witnessing. This passage uses the term "eternal life", and everyone in the conversation needs to understand what this eternal life is.

Immediately, we can observe that the eternal life spoken of here cannot mean endless existence only; that everyone has endless existence and can know it. The context teaches that this eternal life comes through having the Son. Some will not have Him, therefore missing out on eternal life (1 John 5:12). But what do the words "eternal life" mean? Although we could go to John 17:3, which clearly defines eternal life as knowing God and Christ, we would then have to leave the passage, and doing so will not have the same effect as finding our definition within the immediate context. As we read down to verse 20, we discover the biblical solution. It states: *"And we know that the Son of God is come, and hath given us an understanding, that we may know Him that is true, and we are in Him that is true, even in His Son Jesus Christ. This is the true God, and eternal life"* (emphasis mine). This very same chapter we are studying defines eternal life. John tells us that eternal life is being in the One who is true (God the Father) and in His Son, Jesus Christ.

At this point in the discussion, we absolutely must focus on the fact that a person can know objectively that he has eternal life. Here is an example of a conversation in which Mr. Christian shares this concept with Mr. Religious. This conversation is only a pattern to follow, not an exact formula. Witnessing involves flexibility, not rigid form.

MR. CHRISTIAN: What we have read in 1 John 5:13 is very important; we can know that we have eternal life. Because of what God has said, I know I have eternal life. I know I will be with God when I die. Sir, do you know that you will be with God when you die?

MR. RELIGIOUS: (Replies.)

(If he says that he does not know for sure, point out that the Bible says that he can know for certain from 1 John 5:13, and share the grace of God with him. If he says that he does know, and you will have some say so, then ask the following.)

MR. CHRISTIAN: In order to understand what you mean by saying that you are certain of eternal life, may I ask you an important question?

MR. RELIGIOUS: Yes.

MR. CHRISTIAN: If I were to join your organization or church, what is the minimum amount of requirements I must meet in order to get to the best God would have for me?

(Or – What is the least I would have to do to get to your highest level?) [10]

MR. RELIGIOUS: (Replies.)

(If he cannot give you a list, then share with him that he cannot really know he will make it to God, because he does not know how much he must do. Remind him that God says you can know you have eternal life. If he does give you a list, help him with it. Ask him if church membership, baptism, communion, missionary work, tithing, good works, and anything else you can recall are necessary. If he says that any of these works are not necessary, ask him if he will make it to God without doing the "unnecessary" thing if it is within his power to do. Help him to make the list as long as possible. What you are doing is helping this individual to realize, perhaps for the first time, how much he believes he needs to do to reach God. The bigger the list, the more difficult and ridiculous the task of earning one's salvation will become. Once you have established the list, ask the following question.)

MR. CHRISTIAN: Have you done everything on your list?

(This question is very fair if his list is an accurate reflection of what he believes and if he claims that he knows he has eternal life based on it.)

MR. RELIGIOUS: (Replies.)

(If he has not done all the things on his list for salvation, then by his own standards, he cannot know he has eternal life. In fact, he must be lost. Yet, God says that you can know you have eternal life and be with Him. If the individual with whom you are talking says that he has done everything on the list, ask him this last question.)

MR. CHRISTIAN: Can you guarantee me beyond all possible doubt that you will always continue to do everything on your list?

MR. RELIGIOUS: (Replies.)

(If he is intellectually honest, he cannot make such a guarantee. No one could. Any individual can choose to do wrong at any time, and he would be guilty of gross religious arrogance to state otherwise. When

123

he admits this lack, remind him that he cannot know he has eternal life if he can lose it, for eternal life by its very nature cannot be lost. It is not temporary life; it is eternal life. If he does not know that he has eternal life through his works, then why does 1 John 5:13 say that knowing certainly is possible? The stage is set once again to share the gospel and why you know that you have eternal life.)

The value of 1 John 5:9-13 is not limited to any particular cult or religion. It is a profitable passage to share with anyone. Because of that universality, let's review this important set of possible witnessing questions based on these verses one more time.

Question: Do you know that you have eternal life? Do you know that you will be with God the Father when you die? OR Do you know that you will have God's very best when you die?

Listen to Response. (If he does not know that he has eternal life, then what he believes disagrees with the Bible, for the Bible says that you can know. He then must choose between what he believes and the Bible.)

Question: If I were to join your church (or religious group or organization), what is the very least I would have to do to make it to your highest level?

Listen to Response. (If he does not know the least, how can he know if he has done enough? If he does give you a list, then help him with it. Get it as big as he will let you.)

Question: Have you done your list?

Listen to Response. (If he has not done his list, then by his own standards, he will not reach God. If he claims he has done all on his list, then ask the following.)

Question: Can you guarantee me that you will always do everything on your list?

Listen to Response. (If he cannot guarantee that he will always do every item, then something could happen along the way to cause him to lose his salvation.)

How can we know that we have eternal life while our religious friends are unable to know? Our salvation does not depend on a list. It depends on Christ!

Leading the person with whom you are talking to the Lord at this point in the discussion is a wonderful experience. If you are unable to do so, however, end the discussion as a concerned friend, keeping the door open for yourself or the next person God brings into his or her life. Remember, God's work is not limited to just one conversation!

Five

Biblical Authority

The next few chapters, which are written in direct, concise, research format, are designed to facilitate the learning process as well as to provide quick, easy reference to information needed to witness effectively. This part of the book will provide a convenient resource for serious students as they face a multitude of problems in communicating Christ to cult members and other religious people. The subjects listed here might be viewed as a theology digest, but in an easy-to-read style. While covering every area is impossible to do, the subjects addressed here are the most common. The main points are in alphabetical order in chapters five through eight.

The Bible Stands Alone

Realizing why the Bible is the only Word of God that God has given is very important from a biblical standpoint. Many groups today do not believe that the Bible is complete. They may add to it in the form of additional "scripture" or lay claim to having a living prophet among them. You will also hear claims that the Bible has become corrupt through the centuries, that a total apostasy from the truth has taken place. Therefore, according to some cults, they need to correct the Bible so that we will have an accurate translation. Discovering what the Bible teaches about itself is one of the most important quests for truth on which we can embark. In working with groups such as Mormons that believe in additional scripture beyond the Bible, a twofold approach has proven to be quite effective. First, demonstrate that the Bible is complete and that we do not need additional revelation. If the cult insists on additional revelation, go to approach number two, which is as follows. Even if revelation did exist today, it could not exist on the basis that the truth of God was lost and needed to be restored. The following explanation gives the reasons why.

The Bible Alone Is Our Authority

The Bible teaches everything we need to know about God (2 Timothy 3:15-16). It teaches salvation through faith (v. 15) as well as doctrine and how to be right with God (v. 16). The record of God is more certain than the testimony of men (1 John 5:9-11). Once Scripture came into being, it was more sure than a supposed vision from heaven (2 Peter 1:16-21). In fact, Paul warned against claims of angelic visitors from heaven in Galatians 1:8-9.

The Bible Is Without Error

The Bible does not need to be corrected (Psalm 12:6-7). God's truth (the Bible) does not need to be restored, because God's truth can never be lost. (Some verses in the Bible speak of apostasy, but no verses teach a total apostasy.)

1. God's truth endures to all generations (Psalm 100:5).
2. God's words will be in the mouths of His people always to all generations (Isaiah 59:21). This verse means that God's truth will endure not just for all generations up in heaven, but also here on the earth as well.
3. The Word of God cannot become corrupt (1 Peter 1:23).
4. The gates of hell will not prevail against the church (Matthew 16:18). Hence, Satan's attacks against truth will not succeed!

The Bible Is Complete

We do not need additional Scripture. The biblical faith was once for all delivered to the saints (Jude 3). It does not need to be restored over and over again. What the apostles wrote is the foundation of the church age (Ephesians 2:19-20). Just as Jesus would not remain in physical presence with us, neither would the apostles. A foundation does not extend through the whole building but forms the base on which workers construct the building. The apostles' job was to lay the foundation by completing the Word of God (Colossians 1:25). The Greek word here translated "fulfill" means "complete". Once the task of completing the Bible was done, the apostles would be replaced by the Bible. The Bible would then become the hierarchy of the church today in place of the apostles and prophets.

Therefore, by the time of the death of the last apostle (John, as history records) we would have "all truth" of God (John 14:26; 16:13). The night before He was to die, Jesus spoke to the disciples who were to be His apostles. He informed them that, when the Spirit of truth came, He would guide them into all truth. They would be the instruments used to complete God's recorded truth.

The Bible states that there were only twelve apostles (Revelation 21:14). Other people were called apostles (special messengers), but only twelve people were to hold the office. The Bible indicates that one of the requirements of being an apostle is that a person must see Christ personally. This stipulation might very well make Paul the true replacement of Judas (1 Corinthians 9:1). The groups today who claim to have living apostles contradict Scripture.

Some Bible-believing scholars debate whether or not Matthias is the replacement for Judas (Acts 1:20-26). By casting lots, the remaining apostles determined that Matthias should take Judas' place. Were the apostles acting on their own or under the Spirit's guidance? Possibly, God wanted Matthias to be the replacement to Judas as a twelfth apostle to the Jews, therefore making Paul a special apostle to the Gentiles only, not part of the original twelve, nor was he ever meant to be (Acts 26:17; Romans 11:13;

Galatians 2:8; 1 Timothy 2:7). No matter what position a person holds on this point, replacing Judas to allow for twelve apostles to the Jews does not mean that apostles should be replaced in the future. God meant the church to have just twelve apostles. Paul may have been the twelfth or completely separate to the Gentiles as a thirteenth and unique messenger.

With the coming of Christ, the age of the prophets was drawing to a close (Hebrews 1:1-2). The book of Hebrews is a book of comparisons. It compares many aspects of the Old Testament with the New and presents Jesus as the better solution than what the Old offered. Jesus is better than the sacrifices, better than the priests, better than the prophets. The prophets were needed until the time of Christ, and then that necessity changed. The apostles' job was to record the words of Christ and His better doctrine (John 14:26; 16:13-14; Acts 26:16). This record would complete the revelation process with the completed Scripture.

Some in various Christian groups and cults try to take Amos 3:7 and use it to prove the need for prophets today. The verse reads, *"Surely the Lord God will do nothing, but He revealeth His secret unto His servants the prophets."* We do not deny God's use of men to reveal His truth (2 Peter 1:21), but a time came when God had revealed all that He wanted man to know. Again, Scripture is more sure than visions (2 Peter 1:18-20).

Another claim made for the need of prophets and apostles uses Ephesians 4:11-13. *"And He gave some, apostles; and some, prophets; and some, evan-*

gelists; and some, pastors, and teachers; For the perfecting of the saints, for the work of the ministry, for the edifying of the body of Christ: Till we all come in the unity of the faith, and of the knowledge of the Son of God, unto a perfect man, unto the measure of the stature of the fulness of Christ." The question is: "Have we come into the unity of the faith?" In one sense, we have. Verse fourteen tells us that when this unity of the faith and knowledge is here, we will not be tossed about by every false doctrine that comes along. In other words, we will have at our disposal the means to know the truth. How will we know true doctrine? The written Word of God is the answer (2 Timothy 3:16). Whatever "unity of the faith" means, nothing in this passage dictates the time length each of the given offices will last. God gave us the collective package of apostles, prophets, evangelists, pastors, and teachers to bring us to this "unity of the faith." Ephesians 2:20 clearly indicates that the apostles and prophets were foundational and that we should build upon their work. The blocks added to this building were the evangelists, pastors, and teachers.

Apostles and prophets were to give revelation, while the evangelists, pastors, and teachers were to instruct us in the revelation given. Each one does his part (Ephesians 4:16). When the revelation was complete, apostles and prophets would cease to be. They were no longer needed. Evangelists, pastors, and teachers would, by their very nature, continue. Also, if "unity of the faith" means the second coming of Christ as some (e.g. Mormons) claim, then the logical conclusion is that we could experience no total apostasy, for the divine offices of verse 11 (at least some of them) would have to continue until the coming of Christ. This logic also would destroy the Mormon position that these divine offices ceased to exist in their entirety and had to be restored.

Finally, Scripture tells us not to add or take away from God's Word (Revelation 22:18-19). I believe that God placed these words in the last part of the last book of the Bible for a reason, not by accident. I would caution anyone, however, against using this passage as a proof text that the Bible is complete, especially in dealing with the cults. They will reply that this verse is a particular warning given for the book of Revelation, and they are technically right. They will also point out the two other times in Scripture when God gives us just such a warning (Deuteronomy 4:2 and Proverbs 30:5-6). Their question is: "Do you stop Scripture being given at Deuteronomy or Proverbs? If not, what gives you the right to stop it at Revelation?" This counter logic is not unreasonable, but we need to realize that the Deuteronomy and Proverbs passages actually complement the Revelation verses. We should never add to or take away from God's Word. The Revelation verses are not the best references to prove that the Bible is complete, but they do indicate so. Other verses that we examined earlier in this chapter state the same truth better and more clearly.

Bible versus the Book of Mormon

We see various references in the Bible to prophets being given books by God (Ezekiel 2:9) and/or seeing books in a vision (Isaiah 29:4, 11-14). The Mormons claim that these verses refer to the *Book of Mormon*. The answer to that claim rests in the context where the verses appear. In the majority of cases, the Old Testament verses used by the Mormons to "prove" their claim that the *Book of Mormon* is referenced actually deal directly with the nation of Israel, both in the immediate sense and prophetically. No reason exists to single out the *Book of Mormon* as the prophetic fulfillment. If the passages were referring to a future divine book, why not the Koran or other "scriptures" men have produced throughout history? One might even make the claim that the Old Testament is referring to the New. The best answer is that these references are illustrations God uses to present His particular point in the passage under question and that these references should be confined to the subject being discussed in the passage. The point of the verses in Ezekiel 2 was that God's message was so complete that it filled a scroll front and back, something that was not usually done. The point of the verses in Isaiah 29 is that God will reveal His working not to those who seem qualified to know but to those whom He chooses.

The two sticks in Ezekiel 37:15-20 are another attempt by the Mormons to claim that the Bible points to the *Book of Mormon*. These two sticks are supposed to be, according to the Mormons, illustrative representatives of the Bible and the *Book of Mormon*, indicating that the two "scriptures" would eventually be one. Actually, the next two verses (Ezekiel 37:21-

22) teach that the two sticks are, instead, the nations of Judah and Israel.

Finally, the Mormons say the phrase "other sheep" of John 10:16 applies to the Jewish people (house of Israel) who, they claim, came to the American continent in the *Book of Mormon* story. But the context (John 9:13-10:39) actually teaches that Christ was speaking to the house of Israel. He was informing them that He had other sheep that were not of the house of Israel, not Jewish! Who? The Gentiles who would believe on Him!

Priesthood and Authority

As we shared earlier, the authority of men in the form of the apostles and prophets has been replaced with the authority of the Bible. This replacement brings us to the issue of divine authority once given to men found in the Old Testament priesthood. The question is: does that same authority exist today? Priesthood is linked with authority not only in the cults, but also among other "Christian" religions. This issue is very serious because the authority of modern religious priesthood gives the religious leaders, within their doctrine, divine control of the Word of God and of their followers. To counter their concepts, we must know what biblical priesthood was and is all about. The main issues are:

1. What is the difference between the Aaronic priesthood and the Melchisedec priesthood?
2. Is every believer a priest, or do special priesthood offices exist today?

The Aaronic Priesthood

These priests were of the tribe of Levi (Hebrews 7:5). Any claim to the Aaronic priesthood must come from a Levite Jew. The main responsibility of these priests was to intercede for the sins of the people of Israel by presenting the blood of slain animals within the veil of the temple (Hebrews 9:6-7). If a person claims to be an Aaronic priest, he must perform blood sacrifices. The Levitical Aaronic priesthood had to be transferred from generation to generation, because each generation had the natural and unfortunate habit of dying (Hebrews 7:23).

The Melchisedec Priesthood

Jesus is the only person to be made a priest after the order of (connected to) Melchisedec (Hebrews 7:15-22). Anyone else making the claim cannot be biblical. Jesus, our Melchisedec Priest, offered Himself as the blood sacrifice (Hebrews 9:11-12). He replaced the need for the Aaronic priests because He was the complete and successful sacrifice once and for all (Hebrews 9:25-28). Christ not only is the only priest linked with Melchisedec, but He also replaced the Aaronic priests (who could not live forever, but died), because Jesus will continue forever in His priesthood position. It will not be given to another (Hebrews 7:24). The word "unchangeable" in the King James Version is "intransmissible" in the Greek. This office will not change from one person to the next. Anyone claiming to have any special priesthood office must also claim that Christ was removed from His priesthood.

The Christian Priesthood

When Christ died, the veil of the temple, through which only the high priest could enter the presence of God, was torn in two, top to bottom (Matthew 27:51). This act signified that the way into God's presence was open to anyone who came to God through Jesus Christ (John 14:6). Because a priest was the only one who could enter before, this opening made all believers priests in their ability to interact with God. Peter taught that every believer holds such a royal priesthood position (1 Peter 2:5-9).

Sign Gifts and Prophecy

One of the most controversial discussions today deals with sign gifts, and perhaps the most controversial verse in that discussion is 1 Corinthians 13:8. The verse reads, *"Charity never faileth: but whether there be prophecies, they shall fail; whether there be tongues, they shall cease; whether there be knowledge, it shall vanish away."*

Unquestionably, this passage teaches that these three things will come to an end. The use of prophecy will have no purpose. The gift of special languages will stop. Knowledge as a unique and divine gift will not be given any longer. When and what Paul is talking about become the crucial questions. I will not pretend that I have the final answers on this discussion, but I will share what I believe to be biblical on this emotionally charged subject.

Let's examine more closely these three items that God says will come to an end. Prophecy was the giving forth of truth by divine revelation. The gift of languages was a sign to prove that the message was from God and therefore needed an interpreter (1 Corinthians 14:27-28). Obviously, knowledge and the ability to know and understand will not come to an end someday (1 Corinthians 13:12). This reference to knowledge in 1 Corinthians 13:8 probably refers to the "word of knowledge" found in 1 Corinthians 12:8, which involved special divine understanding. Therefore, the conclusion is that all three of these gifts have to do with God giving divine revelation.

Mark 16:20 teaches that God designed sign gifts to authenticate His revelations to humanity. Paul taught that the Jews in particular seek a sign (1 Corinthians 1:22). Peter and the others healed the sick and cast out demons because they had special gifts to prove that they were receiving revelation from God. The logical conclusion is that, when God no longer gave revelation to people (i.e. at the completion of the Bible) we would no longer need to prove that the revelations were from Him, and the sign gifts that did so would stop. You do not put a fork in your mouth without food (normally), nor do you have a sign gift to prove that you are receiving revelation if no revelation is being given.

Is God able to do miraculous things in our time? The answer is, of course, yes! Could God heal somebody, cause a demon to leave a person, or enable one person to understand another even though they do not speak the same language? Of course, God is still God and not limited by theological systems. But God also is logical and keeps His Word. If God chooses to do these things today, His intervention will not be based on a person having the gift to do so, but because God in His sovereignty has decided to extend extraordinary grace. His intervention would not be a gift given to a man to use when that man decided, as the apostles did.

Part of the discussion that centers on 1 Corinthians 13: 8 touches verses 9 and 10: *"For we know in part, and we prophesy in part. But when that which is perfect is come, then that which is in part shall be done away."* The issue is: what is the perfect thing that is coming?

Is it Christ? In a way, that assumption seems logical because verse 12 refers to seeing oneself face to face as we truly are. The difficulty is that the perfect thing is in the neuter and not masculine in the Greek. For Paul to use that gender if he were talking about his Lord would be unusual. One possible way that he might use the neuter form would be if he were referring to the event of Christ's coming, not the person of Christ. This conclusion seems to stretch the whole concept quite a bit. (The reason some would like to make 1 Corinthian 13:10 refer to Christ is that they could then argue that prophecy, tongues, and special knowledge will continue until the coming of Christ.)

Is the perfect thing love? Love would fit contextually. The main emphasis of the chapter is the supremacy and power of love, but is Paul saying that, when love comes, prophecy, special languages, and special knowledge will cease? Would these gifts not already have ceased then with the first coming of Christ or at least with the coming of the Holy Spirit to the church on Pentecost? Does not Christ or the Holy Spirit bring perfect love? Most likely, Paul was not referring to love in verses 8–12, but to something else that would illustrate that the much sought after gifts of prophecy, special languages, and special knowledge were only temporary, making love the center of spiritual focus, where it should be.

So what was the perfect thing Paul was talking about? I believe that most probably Paul was sharing that the completed Bible would be the perfect thing that would replace the gifts of prophecy, special languages, and special knowledge, allowing us to see ourselves as we truly are, with the complete understanding of ourselves that God would have us know. What Paul was saying is: don't center your life on miraculous sign gifts that are about to be replaced with the completed Bible. Instead, center your life on God's love, which is not focused on self and one's ability to do the miraculous, but is focused on extending and demonstrating Christ to others.

Six

Deity Described

God

Several key areas concerning who God is and what He is like have come under attack by the cults and some religions. What does the Bible teach in these areas?

Only One God

> *"For thus saith the LORD that created the heavens; God Himself that formed the earth and made it...I am the LORD; and there is none else"* (Isaiah 45:18).
>
> *"Look unto Me, and be ye saved, all the ends of the earth: for I am God, and there is none else"* (Isaiah 45:22).

Many cults and religions (including some that claim to be Christian) teach that multiple deities exist. For example, many groups within the New Age Movement believe (in various ways) that beings evolved somewhere in time and space and achieved a form of deity. They are now available to assist others in the process, at least the good deities are. The bad ones are a different story. Another example is the Mormon Church, which claims to be Christian. As shared earlier, this cult teaches the existence of many gods in the universe who produce men who become gods who then in turn produce more men, etc. Once again, in review, this line of succession includes God the Father as well. Mormons believe that our God was once a man who earned godhood, just as they hope to do. So what do they do about the Bible verses that teach only one God?

The Mormons argue that the verses referring to only one God mean that we deal with only one God for our earth, and that other deities reign elsewhere in the universe. This argument, however, ignores the literal, common sense understanding of the verses. On occasion, Mormons with whom I have talked about this subject have used the following illustration to try to prove their position. God says in Exodus 20:13, "Thou shalt not kill," yet in Genesis 9:6, He gives an exception. Therefore, when the Bible says that God is the only God, there can be an exception. This kind of Mormon logic is misleading if not thought through carefully. Had God said, "Thou shalt not kill under any circumstances," then He could have allowed no exceptions; but He did not say so. In the area of God being the only God, He did in no uncertain terms say that He was the only God. *"Know therefore this day, and consider it in thine heart, that the LORD He is God in heaven above, and upon the earth beneath: there is none else"* (Deuteronomy 4:39). A question to ask a Mormon is: "If God was indeed the only God in the entire universe and wanted you to know, how would He express that message?" Just about any way the Mormon replies appears in the Bible.

Consider this thought: if other gods were in the universe, certainly God would know about them, but He states that He knows of no others (Isaiah 44:8). (All these responses are valid, not only with Mormons, but with others groups that have multiple deities. We must remember, however, that all groups may not initially accept the Bible as an authority.)

No One Else Can Become a God

Not only do many cults and religions teach about multiple deities, many also teach that people can become deities. The Mormon concept of exaltation described in the previous point illustrates this teaching. Mormon doctrine (or concepts) teaches that the main purpose of our existence is to become a god. This idea is not new at all. The temptation to be like God was the downfall of Satan (Isaiah 14:14). And Satan used this same lie in the Garden of Eden with Eve (Genesis 3:5). It worked then, and it continues to succeed for our spiritual adversary in religions around the world.

God's counter-argument is very simple. He said that there could be no gods before or after Him (Isaiah 43:10). Despite the straightforward statement just referenced, Mormons and others use misunderstood verses to prove the concept of multiple gods.

In John 10:34: *"Jesus answered them, Is it not written in your law, I said, Ye are gods?"* Jesus could not have meant that the religious hypocrites to whom He was speaking were gods. (The Mormons who use this verse ignore their theological teaching that we cannot become gods in this life, but only in the resurrection.) What did Jesus mean? First, He was quoting Psalm 82:6. If we were to examine this Psalm closely, we would discover that all of Psalm 82 deals with judgment. The people referenced in Psalm 82 had become as gods to Israel because of the position God gave them to judge Israel. The name for gods is *elohim*, meaning "strong ones." It is a term often used for God throughout the Old Testament; hence, we see its translation as "gods" in this verse. When it appears as a title for God, it is usually in the plural form, a grammatical shift which emphasizes the multiple greatness of the one true God. Secondly, in John 10:30-39, Jesus is making a strong statement in regard to His deity. If God would call mere men gods because of their power and authority, how much more appropriately does Christ take the title of "Son of God", as He was and is God the Son, actual deity?

1 Corinthians 8:5-6: *"For though there be that are called gods, whether in heaven or in earth, (as there be gods many, and lords many,) but to us there is but one God, the Father, of whom are all things, and we in Him; and one Lord Jesus Christ, by whom are all things, and we by Him."* The context teaches

that the gods and lords here are idols created by man. There is only one God (1 Corinthians 8:4).

God Is Not Changing or Evolving

> *"Before the mountains were brought forth, or ever thou hadst formed the earth and the world, even from everlasting to everlasting, thou art God"* (Psalm 90:2).
> *"For I am the LORD, I change not; therefore ye sons of Jacob are not consumed"* (Malachi 3:6).

More than one religious group holds the concept of an evolving God. Yet the Bible teaches that God, in the person of Jesus Christ, is the same yesterday, today, and forever (Hebrews 13:8). If God were evolving, He would not be complete at this moment. He would not be all He one day will be; therefore, He would now be in a state of deficiency. This idea contradicts Scripture, because the Bible identifies God as the Almighty and absolute (Revelation 1:8).

God Is Not By Nature a Man

As stated earlier, Mormon doctrine teaches that God was once a man. Romans 1:21-24 carries a serious warning about making God into the image of man.

God in essence is deity, not human by nature. The very concept of an absolute, Supreme Being teaches this principle (see Numbers 23:19 and Hosea 11:9). God is not and never was a man; except, of course, when the second person of the Godhead was born here on earth as our Lord Jesus Christ. The absolute nature of who God is makes the fact of God coming in the flesh (in the person of Jesus Christ) even more miraculous.

God Does Not Have a Body

The fact that God created us in His image (Genesis 1:27) does not mean that He looks like us or we look like Him. The Bible teaches that the image of God comes from being created in righteousness and holiness (Ephesians 4:24) as well as being created in knowledge (Colossians 3:10). God's likeness is identified with righteousness (Psalm 17:15). The image of God that Adam and Eve lost in the Garden of Eden was the holiness of God, the righteousness of God, and the knowledge of God. Only the Lord of Glory could repair such damage.

God exists in His natural essence as a Spirit Being (John 4:24). Jesus stated that a being which exists as a spirit does not have a body of flesh and bones (Luke 24:39). For a being that exists in spiritual essence to have a physical body is not normal. This statement does not contradict the facts that Jesus is indeed God in the flesh (1 Timothy 3:16; John 1:14) and that the only way anyone has seen God is through the person of Christ (John 1:18; 14:9). Christ shared the statement in Luke 24:39 to help the disciples understand that He was physically resurrected. The natural state of God is spiritual in essence. The only way God can be said to have a body is that God the Son now has a body.

Mormons, for example, try to prove that God has a body by quoting verses that speak of the hand, arm, or eyes of God. That same logic, if followed to its logical conclusion, can be used to show that God is a bird (Psalm 91:4). Of course, God is not a bird, but the Bible does use figurative language, such as hand, arm, or eyes, to describe characteristics of God, such as protection, strength, or knowledge.

Finally, if God had a body, He could be seen, but the Bible teaches that God is invisible (1 Timothy 1:17).

Holy Spirit

Many religious groups reduce the Holy Spirit to being just a force or movement of whatever their view of deity is. The Mormons add a unique twist by making the claim that the Holy Spirit ("the Father's influence") and the Holy Ghost ("a person") are different, because the King James translation uses both phrases; yet, Spirit and Ghost are translations of the same Greek word, *pneuma*. Different committees of translators doing different passages chose different English words to translate the same Greek word. This variation doesn't mean that either team of translators was wrong. In fact, both groups of translators were basically right. The word *pneuma* can be translated "spirit" or "ghost". Most modern translations now choose to use the word "spirit" as the consistent translation.

The Holy Spirit Is a Person

The Bible teaches that the Holy Spirit possesses intellect (1 Corinthians 12:8), will (1 Corinthians 12:11), and emotions (Ephesians 4:30). These qualities are characteristics of a person, not an influence. Scripture gives Him designations proper to a personality (John 14:16-17). Associations of His name show that He is a person (John 16:14; Acts 15:28). The Holy Spirit performs acts proper to a personality (Ephesians 4:30). He is clearly distinguished from His gifts (Luke 1:35; 4:14; Romans 8:26; 1 Corinthians 12:8).

The Holy Spirit Is God

Peter used a comparative principle of logic when he informed Ananias that, in lying to the Holy Spirit, Ananias was indeed lying to God (Acts 5:3-4).

The Holy Spirit Is Received at Salvation

We receive the Holy Spirit when we receive Christ. Jesus said that the Holy Spirit would act through those who believe in Him (John 7:37-39). If a person does not have Christ's Spirit, he does not belong to Him. Therefore, one must receive the Spirit when he is born into God's family, or he is not part of the family (Romans 8:9). Paul further taught that one receives the Holy Spirit when he trusts in Christ (Ephesians 1:13).

Jehovah

One of the biggest controversies raging between true Christianity and the cults is the question: who is Jehovah? For example, the Mormons teach that Jesus is Jehovah, but God the Father is not. The Jehovah's Witnesses teach that God the Father is Jehovah, but Jesus Christ is not. The fact is that the Bible teaches that God the Father and Jesus, as well as the Holy Spirit, are Jehovah. To set the record straight, we need to realize that the name "Jehovah" is not actually the true name of God. The Hebrew language did not have any vowels in its original form; therefore, the actual name of God was *YHWH* or, transliterated another way into English, JHVH. The Jewish scribes, out of respect for God, did not want to pronounce His name in oral readings; so they said *Adonai* (the Hebrew word for Lord or Master) instead. Eventually, scholars added vowel markings to the Hebrew consonants; but when the scholars came to the name of God, *YHWH*, they inserted the vowel markings for *Adonai* instead. The scholars did so in order to prompt the scribe reading the text aloud to say *Adonai* instead of the actual holy name of God. The result was *Yehowah* or *Jehovah*. Most scholars agree today that probably the actual name for God is *Yahweh*, but we cannot be certain. These variations appear as if God on purpose protected His name from those who would defile it.

For simplicity's sake, in this book we will continue to use the combination/traditional word *Jehovah* to refer to the Hebrew name of God, *Yahweh*. We have chosen to do so because of the common usage of "Jehovah" in Bible discussion and research, especially among cults and particularly the Jehovah's Witnesses.

As you examine the following verses, particularly note the way the King James translators showed the Hebrew names for God in their English translation of the Old Testament. (This practice is true of many modern translations as well.) Note the use of lowercase and uppercase letters in the words below. The translators deliberately wrote these names this way so that you would know what Hebrew word they had translated into English. Now when you see Lord GOD or LORD God combinations, as well as the words Lord/LORD or God/GOD, you will know what Hebrew names writers of Scripture used for God.

God – *Elohim*
Lord – *Adonai*
LORD or GOD – *Jehovah*

Father Is Jehovah

Jehovah (LORD) says to Jesus Christ (Lord), "Sit thou at my right hand" (Psalm 110:1). Clearly, God the Father makes this statement. Jehovah (LORD) places our sin on Jesus Christ (Isaiah 53:6); God the Father clearly performs this action.

Jesus Christ Is Jehovah

Jehovah (LORD) states that His cost was thirty pieces of silver (Zechariah 11:13). Judas's betrayal of Christ fulfilled this prophecy (Matthew 26:14-16). Jehovah (LORD) was to be pierced (Zechariah 12:4, 10). Christ also fulfilled this prophecy in His death (John 19:34). Jesus states that He is the I AM (John

8:58). Only Jehovah Elohim (LORD God) could make such a claim (Exodus 3:14-15).

Holy Spirit Is Jehovah

In Psalm 95, Jehovah (LORD) warns His people not to test Him as their fathers did (Psalm 95:6-11). The writer of Hebrews says that the Holy Spirit was speaking when Jehovah gave that warning (Hebrews 3:7-11). We can use the same procedure with Jeremiah 31:33 and Hebrews 10:15-16.

Jesus Christ

The Bible teaches us that we can know if a group of individuals are true believers by comparing their Jesus with the Jesus of the Bible (1 John 4:1-3). Who, then, is the biblical Christ?

Jesus Is Not an Angel

Very few cults avoid the doctrinal error of concluding that Jesus was a created being or angel. Once again, this concept comes from misunderstanding Scripture. The Bible teaches clearly that Jesus is not a created angelic being (Micah 5:2).

The Bible also teaches that Christ is the firstborn (Colossians 1:15). Therefore, according to many cults, He had a beginning. He was the first creature to be "born." This misunderstanding is a result of ignorance of Old Testament customs and how they, under God's direction, influenced New Testament writers. Jesus holds the "firstborn" position or headship position, which gives Him the authority over the household of the Father. This position does not mean that He is a created being. Colossians 1:18 further clarifies "firstborn" by stating that Jesus was foremost and first to be resurrected.

In the King James Version, Jesus states in Revelation 3:14 that He is the "beginning" of God's creation. This statement does not mean that Christ was the first object to be created by God. Instead, Paul taught that all creation finds its origin in Christ (Colossians 1:16).

We should not take passages such as John 10:29, which state in essence, "My Father...is greater than all," to mean that the Father is more powerful or "more God" than Jesus Christ. Such passages do state the relationship within the being of God. Here we encounter an issue not of equality, but of functionality. The three persons of the being of God are equal, but they function in a proper order. One could also understand this verse to express the relationship of the Father to His Son in regard to Christ's earthly ministry, where the Man Christ Jesus totally submitted to the will of the Father.

Jesus is the "only begotten" (John 3:16), but not because He had a beginning. Jesus was the only One to come from the presence of God the Father (John 3:13) to be uniquely born ("only begotten") of the virgin, having been conceived by the Holy Spirit (Luke 1:35).

Jesus Is God

Thomas believed that Jesus was God, or he would never have called Him God, a statement no Jew would make casually without firm conviction

(John 20:28). God the Father also identifies Christ as God (Hebrews 1:8). God the Father would obviously know!

The apostle John states clearly that the Word of whom he speaks in chapter one of his gospel account is God (see verse one. A special section in the chapter "Practical Responses" later in this book will deal with the Jehovah's Witnesses' position regarding John 1:1.) For now, we want to compare Scripture to demonstrate that Jesus is the Word, and the Word is God. Therefore, Jesus is God.

1. The Word was made flesh (John 1:14). Jesus is God in the flesh (1 Timothy 3:16).
2. The Word is the "only begotten" (John 1:14). The "only begotten" is Jesus Christ (John 1:18).
3. The Word is King of Kings and Lord of Lords (Revelation 19:13, 16). Jesus Christ is Kings of Kings and Lord of Lords (1 Timothy 6:14-15).

Jesus Is Not the Brother of Satan

The Mormon doctrine that Jesus is the brother of Satan is a somewhat twisted version of the idea that Jesus is an angel. The concept is that Jesus, Satan, and all the rest of us were once spirit children in heaven (one of the many versions of angels in Mormon theology) born literally to God the Father through his wife or wives. The Christian response to the doctrine that Jesus and Satan are brothers rests on the same biblical truths which demonstrate that Jesus is not an angel. Satan was created (Ezekiel 28:13), and Jesus wasn't created. He is God. (This fact has been demonstrated earlier in this chapter.)

Jesus Was Physically Resurrected

The resurrection of Christ is part of the gospel message (1 Corinthians 15:1-4). The resurrection cannot be separated from the gospel, despite the fact that some groups try. Without Christ's resurrection, we have no hope for our salvation (1 Corinthians 15:12-19). This resurrection of our Lord was not just a spiritual resurrection but an actual, physical resurrection of His flesh and bone body (Luke 24:39).

Trinity

The word "Trinity" does not occur in the Bible. It is simply a theological term that describes a biblical fact. The doctrine teaches that God is one being who exists as three persons. Each person is distinct, but all three exist as one God. People have tried to analyze this doctrine unnecessarily. God by His very nature of being God exists as three persons. To question why God exists as three persons is just as absurd as questioning why a man has two arms instead of four. Man by his natural existence has two arms. God by His natural existence is three persons.

The Trinity can be demonstrated scripturally by placing verses which teach that each person of the Godhead is God beside verses which teach that only one God exists. (We explained both of these doctrines earlier in the chapter.) Conclusion: the Father is God; the Son is God; the Holy Spirit is God;

and there is only one God. Therefore, God exists as three persons.

Two Important References

Along with the practical method described above to demonstrate God's existence as a three-person being, additional, more direct Trinity passages appear in Scripture. We will look at two of them here. One appears in the Old Testament, and one in the New.

The first one is the Old Testament reference of Isaiah 48:16. In this passage, Jehovah is speaking, and Jehovah states that Jehovah (GOD) and His Spirit have sent Him. This phrasing clearly demonstrates that the singular being of Jehovah exists as three individual persons. To prove that the speaker is Jehovah, compare Isaiah 48:12, in which the speaker says, *"I am the first, I am also the last,"* with Isaiah 44:6, where Jehovah (LORD) states that He is the first and the last. Therefore, the speaker must be Jehovah. (See explanation in this chapter under the section "Jehovah" about the King James translation of LORD or GOD for the word "Jehovah.")

The second reference is in the New Testament in Matthew 28:19. The key to understanding why this reference so absolutely teaches the Trinity is the fact that the verse says "name," not "names" for God (i.e. Father, Son, and Holy Spirit). Therefore, the singular name of the one true God is the Father, the Son, and the Holy Spirit, a three-part name which reflects who He is by nature.

Other Important References

Deuteronomy 6:4 proclaims: *"Hear, O Israel: The LORD our God is one LORD."* In this passage, the Hebrew word for "one" means "a united one". The word translated "LORD" is "Jehovah," meaning the singular, eternal, self-existing One. The word translated "God" is "Elohim," meaning plural, majestic deity (or sometime deities when used to refer to idols). Genesis 1:26 demonstrates this meaning of plural, majestic deity when God refers to Himself as "Us" in the plural. Interestingly enough, there are two plural versions of this word. One is for a plurality of two, and the other is for a plurality of at least three. "Elohim" is the one that means a plurality of at least three. (This word choice is another strong statement of the nature of the triune God.)

So let's put all the words together with their actual meanings and see what we have: **Hear, O Israel: The singular, eternal, self-existing One, our plural, majestic Deity who is at least three, is one singular, eternal, self-existing One.** Wow!

Now, let's turn to another important passage. In John 10:30, Jesus states, *"I and my Father are one."* This passage does not mean one in purpose, as some cults would like to claim, but rather one in essence. Both the Father and the Son are God in their very essence. (Many cults try to make the passage in John 17:21-23 show that Christ only meant oneness of purpose. In reality, Jesus was referring in John 17 to our oneness within the body of Christ. He did not say that we would be deity as He and the Father are in oneness, but that, through His indwelling Spirit, we would have deity dwelling within us. The indwelling Holy Spirit would make us one. His presence would result in our unity of thinking and action. Because God exists as one being, He already has unity of thinking and action.)

Finally, we need to examine another passage of Scripture which Christians often use to prove the Trinity. 1 John 5:7 reads: *"For there are three that bear record in heaven, the Father, the Word, and the Holy Ghost: and these three are one."* Impressive as this verse may seem, it will most likely have no real effect on the cults. The problem is that this verse lacks the usual historic manuscript backing. It is not found in the majority of the Greek manuscripts or in the oldest ones. Scholars can make a case for its authenticity, but anyone trying will find the task a difficult one. Regardless of your personal position, you must realize that the cults are aware, in most cases, of the challenges associated with this verse; so they will disregard it. The important point to remember is that plenty of other Trinity verses appear in the Bible. The great truth of who God is does not find its support in only one verse!

Seven

Scriptural Salvation

The importance of focusing on salvation is obvious. How a person is saved from God's judgment and receives eternal life must be seen as the most vital issue of personal existence above all others. To have the Almighty God of the universe angrily responding in wrath toward you because of your sinfulness is not a good thing. Being saved, however, is not the final purpose of life. Bringing God glory is the true reason for human existence. Yet, our salvation is what allows us to fulfill our purpose of glorifying God in holy harmony as opposed to glorifying Him as an object of His wrath. Given the options, I choose holy harmony. Logically, anyone would, but the world is trapped in blindness: not just the blindness of sinful actions, but the blindness of false religious doctrine and practice. Our great challenge is to share the message that God is good and that He has provided salvation for those who will come to Him.

So now let's study our way through scriptural salvation and examine the various doctrines that constitute this great truth. More than any other doctrine, cults and religions must attack the biblical concepts of salvation. The need for eternal rescue by grace demonstrates the very sinfulness of man and the very heart of God for redemption.

Baptism

While mode and method of baptism are important, this section will deal only with the question of whether baptism is necessary to accomplish, in whole or in part, God's plan of salvation. We will look first at often misunderstood verses. Despite the fact that over two hundred clear references to salvation by grace through trust in Christ appear in the Bible, the cults return to the same few verses over and over to prove that works are needed for eternal life. Religious systems, both cultic and otherwise, often use the following seven references to "prove" that we must be baptized to be saved.

Mark 1:4-5

"John did baptize in the wilderness, and preach the baptism of repentance for the remission of sins. And there went out unto him all the land of Judea, and they of Jerusalem, and were all baptized of him in the river of Jordan, confessing their sins."

Although the baptism of John in the Gospel accounts was for the purpose of identifying with Israel and therefore not the same as baptism in Acts and thereafter, it is sometimes used as part of the argument to prove that baptism causes forgiveness of sins. The verse above is an example reference from Mark that is very similar to Luke 3:3. John the Baptist did not teach baptism as a means of receiving forgiveness. Instead, he taught that repentance brought forgiveness of sins. He also taught, however, that a truly repentant person would immediately publicly declare his repentance with action; the repentant individual would be baptized, demonstrating his repentance for forgiveness of sins. He would undergo the baptism of repentance, declaring publicly his sinfulness. This interpretation is consistent with the passage in Matthew 3:11 where John the Baptist states that he baptized with water unto (with reference to) repentance. Baptism was the result of repentance and the forgiveness of sins, not the cause of it.

Mark 16:16

"He that believeth and is baptized shall be saved; but he that believeth not shall be damned."

This verse is one of the main references used to "demonstrate" that baptism is necessary for salvation. While the statement that he who believes and is baptized shall be saved is true, the key to understanding the verse comes in the second phrase. The one who is condemned is the one who does not believe, not the one who is not baptized. An evangelist once gave this illustration for comparison: "The one who gets on the train and sits down will arrive in Los Angeles, but the one who does not get on the train will not arrive." Getting on the train is what determines that the individual will arrive in Los Angeles, not whether he sits down. A person can remain standing and still ride a train, but he will not be the most comfortable. [11] A person can be on his way to heaven because of trust in Christ without being baptized, but he'll lack the joy of being obedient to God in this area. The point is that believing is what determines salvation, not baptism.

John 3:5

"Jesus answered, Verily, verily, I say unto thee, Except a man be born of water and of the Spirit, he cannot enter into the kingdom of God."

Believing that some people claim that the phrase "born of water" means baptism in light of a context that has nothing to do with baptism may seem difficult. Surprising as this interpretation is, a common position among a variety of religions is that this verse describes literal baptismal water. (The chapter does not discuss water baptism until much later, in a totally different context.) So what does the verse teach?

In the Greek, the word for "and" is *kai,* and many good Bible scholars believe that the word *kai* should be translated "even" in this case. This rendering would make the phrase read, "born of water *even* the Spirit." Doctrinally, this wording is consistent with the rest of John's Gospel and the Bible. The thought is also possible that, in light of the use of the word "water" in the Bible to refer to the written Word of God, this verse might be teaching that being cleansed in the second birth comes when the Holy Spirit uses the Word of God to bring us to Christ. Let's take a look at the book of John and the Bible as a whole to see what kind of support is there for these positions.

The context of the Gospel of John reveals that Jesus spoke of the Spirit as living water, which cleanses us at the moment of believing (John 7:37-39). Secondly, Christ teaches us that His Word cleanses us (John 15:3). The rest of the Bible instructs us that the Holy Spirit washes us at the moment of salvation (Titus 3:5) and that the written Word of God cleanses us (Ephesians 5:26). Peter supports this last concept when he writes that we are born again through the Word of God (1 Peter 1:23).

Another view is that the water refers to physical birth (the water breaking) and the Spirit refers to spiritual birth. The argument arises from the context, especially verse 6 of John 3. The reasoning behind the view is this: you must be born physically to get into your earthly family. You must also be born spiritually to get into God's heavenly family. This position is fairly simple to present to cults, and Christians therefore use it often. Believers should do an honest study, however, to arrive at what they conclude to be the biblical interpretation. Whatever position one takes, the important point to realize is that the verse does not refer to baptism.

Acts 2:38

"Then Peter said unto them, Repent, and be baptized every one of you in the name of Jesus Christ for the remission of sins, and ye shall receive the gift of the Holy Ghost."

To understand this verse properly, one needs to realize that the phrase "be baptized...for the remission of sins" is an interjection in the sentence. What Peter said was "Repent, and ye shall receive the gift of the Holy Ghost." He interjected the other phrase concerning baptism, but his main thrust was in the repentance part. (See the section on the Holy Spirit in the previous chapter.) For Peter (and the Jewish way of thinking that demanded visual response concerning any claims of discipleship) to let people know—that, if they came to Christ and had their sins forgiven, true repentance would lead to immediate baptism—would not be out of character. This baptism would not be done to be saved, but to demonstrate true faith.

So what does the phrase "be baptized for the remission (forgiveness) of sins" mean? The Greek word translated "for" is *eis*, which in this case could be properly translated "because." We are baptized because we have remission or forgiveness.

All baptism does is picture for the world what has already taken place inside the person. Unfortunately, in dealing with the cults, you will find that they do not easily accept this view.

One way of understanding the English translation will help clear up the false concept that baptism is necessary for salvation. The proper understanding of the English word "for" in this verse can be illustrated by the phrase "wanted for murder." The person in question is not wanted "in order to" murder someone. He is wanted "because" he murdered someone. We are not baptized in order to receive forgiveness of sins, but because we have received forgiveness already.

The context shows that the people who responded to Peter's message were baptized after they received the Word (Acts 2:41). A person must receive the message of salvation first and then be baptized, not in order to be saved, but as an act of grateful, obedient love because he is saved. Cornelius and his people were baptized after receiving the Holy Spirit (Acts 10:44-48), not in order to receive Him.

Acts 22:16

"And now why tarriest thou? Arise, and be baptized, and wash away thy sins, calling on the name of the Lord."

By studying this verse in relationship to the other Bible passages on this subject, we understand that the washing away of sins is a play on words, which is linked with calling on the name of the Lord, not with being baptized (see Romans 10:13). The Amplified Bible translates the last of the verse "by calling upon His name wash away your sins" (AMP). The footnote explains that this translation is correct because of the adverbial participle of means. The Good News Translation reads, "Get up and be baptized and have your sins washed away by calling on his name" (GNT). Calling on Christ's name is the means through which the two imperatives of baptism and sins forgiven have a right to be. My sins are forgiven because I have called upon the name of the Lord. I am also baptized because I have called upon the name of the Lord. Baptism should be a natural step of one who has just been saved; forgiveness of sins is the automatic result of trusting Christ (Acts 10:43).

Romans 6:4

"Therefore we are buried with Him by baptism into death: that like as Christ was raised up from the dead by the glory of the Father, even so we also should walk in newness of life."

The word "baptize" appears in the English translation in a few other verses. As they are all explained in much the same way, we will deal with just this verse. Remembering that the word "baptism" is not a translation is important. This word is what is known as a transliteration (matching sound for sound the proper letter from one language alphabet to another). "Baptize" is the English transliteration of the Greek word *baptizo*. The literal meaning is to immerse or place one thing in another. Just because "baptize" is used does not mean that it refers to water baptism. Properly translated without transliteration, the verse reads, "Therefore, we are buried with Him by being placed into death." Paul speaks of a spiritual immersion, but he never said or meant anything about water here.

1 Peter 3:21

> *"The like figure whereunto even baptism doth also now save us (not the putting away of the filth of the flesh, but the answer of a good conscience toward God,) by the resurrection of Jesus Christ."*

The verse itself clarifies the meaning, for it says that baptism does not remove the sins of the flesh. Baptism does give the already born-again believer the knowledge that he has been completely obedient to God's wishes as a newly saved person. By being baptized, the new believer is saved from disobedience to God! Some good Bible scholars believe that the phrase "filth of the flesh" means "dirt of the body," but I believe, along with others, that a study of the word "flesh" as used by Peter and the rest of the Bible will discredit that position for this verse (e.g. 1 Peter 4:2). In any case, the point is still the same. Baptism saves one not from his sinfulness but from an uncomfortable conscience toward God.

The illustration used in the passage is Noah's ark (1 Peter 3:20). Just as Noah came forth from the ark to new life, baptism is a picture ("the like figure") of what happens the moment we receive Christ. We come forth from the grave of sin and death to new life.

Proper Biblical Teaching on Baptism

We have spent quite a bit of time examining verses used by false religions to convince others that baptism is necessary for salvation. Now let's take a brief moment to explore scripturally why baptism does not save or bring forgiveness of sins.

1. Salvation is by grace through faith (Ephesians 2:8-9). This verse is just one of hundreds of verses that teach this truth.
2. Baptism is not a part of the true Gospel message of salvation that is biblically linked to the death, burial, and resurrection of Christ (1 Corinthians 1:17; 15:1-4).
3. Forgiveness of sins comes through trust in Christ alone (Acts 10:43).
4. The thief on the cross was not baptized (Luke 23:42-43). The argument that during that dispensation God had not commanded baptism is not valid. John the Baptist had been baptizing.
5. The proper order is to believe on Jesus Christ for salvation, and then to be baptized after one is saved (Acts 8:35-37; 16:30-34).

6. Finally, Jesus was baptized even though He certainly didn't need any sins forgiven (Matthew 3:13-15). He was identifying Himself with the God of Israel, not seeking forgiveness of sins.

Children of God

Some people today, not only in certain cults but also in some denominations of more orthodox Christianity, believe that everyone on earth is a child of God. Religious people may want that concept to be true, but it certainly is not biblical.

Misunderstood Verses

In Acts 17:29, we read: *"Forasmuch then as we are the offspring of God, we ought not to think that the Godhead is like unto gold, or silver, or stone, graven by art and man's device."* Mankind is the offspring of God only in the sense of creation. God created the first man, and we are descendants of that man (Luke 3:38).

Numbers 16:22 states: *"And they fell upon their faces, and said, O God, the God of the spirits of all flesh, shall one man sin, and wilt thou be wroth with all the congregation?"* Again this verse applies to creation, not to a relationship. When the relationship aspect is being expressed, the phrase is "Father of spirits," and it only applies to those who have become sons of God. God only disciplines His sons, no others (Hebrews 12:5-11).

Malachi 2:10 uses the phrase: *"Have we not all one father?"* People often quote this verse to prove that we are all children of God. The next phrase in the verse explains this statement as applying to the creation of mankind: *"Hath not one God created us?"*

Some Are Not Children of God

The Bible teaches that not everyone is a child of God. Jesus informs the Pharisees that they are of their father, the devil (John 8:44). God's wrath will fall on those titled the "children of disobedience" (Colossians 3:6). Before salvation, God identifies us as the "children of wrath" as well as the "children of disobedience" (Ephesians 2:2-3). Paul called Elymas, the sorcerer, a "child of the devil" (Acts 13:10). That denunciation is about as clear a statement as can be made on the issue.

Becoming Children of God

The Bible teaches that each of us can become a child of God only by being born into God's family through faith in Christ. We become children of God when we receive Christ (John 1:12-13). Verse 13 teaches that we are born again at the moment of salvation. Jesus stated, "Except a man be born again, he cannot see the kingdom of God" (John 3:3). The apostle John said, "Whosoever believeth that Jesus is the Christ is born of God" (l John 5:1). One must have a personal trust in Christ to be born again. "For ye are all the children of God by faith in Christ Jesus" (Galatians 3:26). The key words here are "by faith". The "all" of this passage are the Galatian Christians.

Eternal Security

The biblical position that, once a person has been saved by God, that person will always remain saved has been misunderstood, not only by the cults but also by many others. The Bible does not teach the concept that a person is free to sin once he is saved. It does teach that, once a person is saved, he still has the possibility of sinning (and sometimes he will), but the Lord promises to begin the process of removing the desire to sin as the believer grows in Christ (Ephesians 2:10). As stated earlier, our trust is not what saves us, but the person of Christ. Unless Christ can fail, we cannot lose our salvation. Before we look at the biblical reasons why a person who truly trusts Christ to save him cannot lose that salvation, let's spend a few moments once again examining the misunderstood verses that religious individuals use to "prove" that a person can lose that which God has given.

Matthew 24:13

"But he that shall endure unto the end, the same shall be saved."

This verse is the future setting for the tribulation period, during which the Church will be absent (1 Thessalonians 1:10 with Revelation 6:17). The indication is that Jesus is informing Israel that the ones who remain true to God through the tribulation period will escape God's judgment at the end of the tribulation and enter the thousand-year reign of

Christ (Luke 17:34-37). This indication would make Matthew 24:13 an outward description of action and deeds, not an inward reflection of the heart. This verse does not mean that a person could lose his salvation. The biblical principle of 1 John 2:19 is that, if he is truly saved, he will not leave the truth; he will endure unto the end. If he leaves, he was not truly saved.

We also have another way of looking at this passage. Interestingly enough, the word for "saved" can also be translated "delivered". Maybe Jesus was just sharing a basic fact of reality. Those Jewish people who live during this awful time of tribulation should determine to hang on as best they can, because if they do, this terrible time will come to an end, and they will be delivered.

Galatians 5:4

> *"Christ is become of no effect unto you, whosoever of you are justified by the law; ye are fallen from grace."*

To say that this verse means that we can lose our salvation is to take only the phrase "fallen from grace" and ignore the rest of the verse. It is actually teaching that, if one tries to get to God through keeping God's laws, one is leaving the principle of salvation by grace. Romans 11:6 teaches that one cannot mix grace and works to gain salvation. Galatians 5:5 teaches that God's righteousness comes by faith. Verse 5 is the reply to the idea that verse 4 implies loss of salvation.

Hebrews 6:4-6

"For it is impossible for those who were once enlightened, and have tasted of the heavenly gift, and were made partakers of the Holy Ghost, and have tasted the good word of God, and the powers of the world to come, if they shall fall away, to renew them again unto repentance; seeing they crucify to themselves the Son of God afresh, and put him to an open shame."

People often overlook an important issue about this Scripture passage. If these verses taught that one can lose his salvation, they would also teach that one cannot be saved again (reread vv. 4-6). Most religious systems would find this stipulation a problem, because many of them do teach that, when one loses his salvation, he can be saved again. In verse 9, the writer of Hebrews indicates that he is not talking about believers at all in verses 4-6. He states that he is persuaded that the people to whom he is actually writing the Hebrew epistle are not of the type described in verses 4-6 but are believers manifesting the true fruits of salvation.

Christians have different views on what verses 4-6 are actually saying. One explanation is that when a person comes to the point of true repentance under the leading of the Holy Spirit but refuses to accept Christ, that individual can never be brought again to that repentant position. By rejecting Christ after knowing who He is, he has again, in a figurative way,

171

hung Christ on the cross in open shame. Whatever a person determines these verses to teach, one thing is certain. They are not about salvation being lost. Instead, they describe willful human stubbornness.

Hebrews 10:26-29

> *"For if we sin willfully after that we have received the knowledge of the truth, there remaineth no more sacrifice for sins, but a certain fearful looking for of judgment and fiery indignation, which shall devour the adversaries. He that despised Moses' law died without mercy under two or three witnesses: of how much sorer punishment, suppose ye, shall he be thought worthy, who hath trodden under foot the Son of God, and hath counted the blood of the covenant, wherewith he was sanctified, an unholy thing, and hath done despite unto the Spirit of grace?"*

The same approach taken with Hebrews 6:4-6 can be taken here. To understand biblical salvation clearly and reject it does not remove the fact that Christ's substitutionary death is still the only answer. Interestingly enough, a strong implication exists that the phrase "he was sanctified" of verse 29 is referring to Christ, not to the one rejecting the truth. Christ was "set apart from others in holiness" (sanctified) in his death. He wasn't made holy, but he was uniquely holy. Finally, within the passage but just a few verses later, Hebrews 10:39 informs the readers that they are not of the group who draw back after understanding the truth, but are of those who go ahead and trust Christ. Many people come to the edge of salvation but never cross the line.

2 Peter 1:10

> *"Wherefore the rather, brethren, give dili-*
> *gence to make your calling and election sure:*
> *for if ye do these things, ye shall never fall."*

Cults and others claim that this verse teaches that we are the ones who have to keep ourselves saved before God. This position is a direct contradiction of Scripture. Peter uses the word "election" in verse 10. Paul wrote in Romans 8:29-30 that God's sovereign choosing cannot be undone. Whether you believe we choose God because He chose us or He chooses us because we chose Him, Paul's statements make clear that God will bring His elect safely to His presence. So what is the verse saying? Let's examine the context:

1. *Verse 3* – Peter is speaking to Christians: "given...us all things".
2. *Verse 4* – Having already a knowledge of Christ in salvation (see v. 3), we also receive the promises of a new nature and deliverance from the flesh when we receive Christ. We are made "partakers of the divine nature" in the new birth (John 1:12).

3. *Verses 5-7* – "Besides this" or "for this reason": now the emphasis is not on how we receive the divine nature, but how we develop it.

4. *Verse 8* – If one has made the items listed in this passage of Scripture a part of his life, he will not be barren in his Christian life, but fruitful.

5. *Verse 9* – The person of verse 9 is forgiven, but he has forgotten that he was purged from his sin. Therefore, he lives in it.

6. *Verse 10* – Make your salvation a firm, stable, solid experience. Live your Christian life as God has taught in His Word. This practice will keep you from falling into sin. This exhortation has nothing to do with losing your salvation; it deals with experiencing the power of God in your spiritual existence.

7. *Verse 11* – Speaks of entering heaven abundantly. This verse does not mean that those of verse 9 will not enter. They may not, however, enter abundantly (see 1 Corinthians 3:11-15).

2 Peter 2:20-21

"For if after they have escaped the pollutions of the world through the knowledge of the Lord and Savior Jesus Christ, they are again entangled therein, and overcome, the latter end is worse with them than the beginning. For it had been better for them not to have known the way of righteousness, than, after they have known it, to turn from the holy commandment delivered unto them."

This passage seems to match the Hebrews 6 passage with about the same intent. Therefore, many of the principles that clarified the one will help clarify the other. Let's again examine the context:

1. *Verse 1* – "The Lord that bought them." Christ's death is sufficient even for the false prophets and teachers, but that sufficiency does not mean they are saved.
2. *Verse 15* – "Which have forsaken the right way." To forsake something, one has to be aware of its existence, but one is not necessarily a part of it.
3. *Verse 18* – Teaches that those who follow the false teachers do not totally escape the world ("almost" in Greek). They may have come apart from the world, but they return to it.
4. *Verse 20* – They may have a full knowledge of the facts of salvation, even to the point of believing these facts to be true, but as we pointed out in the previous chapter, a big difference lies between just believing Christ can save and trusting Him to do so.
5. *Verse 21* – To reject Christ after fully understanding what He did on the cross is a terrible thing.
6. *Verse 22* – As Dr. Paul Tassell once said, "You can dress up a pig, but it is still a pig." [12]

1 John 1:6-7

> *"If we say that we have fellowship with Him, and walk in darkness, we lie, and do not the truth: but if we walk in the light, as He is in the light, we have fellowship one with another, and the blood of Jesus Christ His Son cleanseth us from all sin."*

Those who believe they can lose their salvation use the argument that the blood of Jesus only cleanses when you are following God, an argument which in and of itself is a paradoxical statement. Why does one need the blood of Christ to cleanse oneself if one is following God? The response often given to this question (by those who believe in the possibility of lost salvation) is that Christ's blood is cleansing the average, everyday sins as a person seeks to serve God. Verse 7, however, says "all sin," meaning every sin a believer commits.

Some also use 1 John 1:9 to support the idea of "on again, off again" salvation. This verse reads, *"If we confess our sins, He is faithful and just to forgive us our sins, and to cleanse us from all unrighteousness."* The thought here is that, if a person fails to confess a sin of which he is aware, he will live in an unforgiven lost state until he does confess, and then his salvation is restored.

Whatever these collections of verses mean, they cannot mean that one can lose his salvation. Why? Because walking in the light does not mean living without sin, for if we are in the light, the blood of

Jesus cleanses us who are in the light completely. In John 1:9 (Gospel account) we learn that Christ is the light of everyone who is born on earth, but only those who are born into God's family will not flee the light (John 3:18-21). To claim you are a child of God and flee the light is to be a liar (I John 1:6). To walk in the light is the natural result and the true reality of being a child of God. Therefore, I John 1:9 is not a condition of God's salvation but the promise of fellowship and deliverance from sin for God's people when they turn to Him. If a true believer sins, he does not have to run from God; he can run to God in the complete assurance of his unconditional acceptance. We have no fear of salvation loss. God will (and is right in doing so) restore fellowship, granting the joy of forgiveness.

Proper Biblical Teaching

1. Eternal life by its very nature is everlasting (John 3:15). If one could lose his salvation, it would be called temporary life instead of eternal life.
2. Jesus stated that those who are His are held in His hand and in God's hand, and no one can pluck them out of Their hands (John 10:27-29). Jesus said "no man," which means everyone, including the person being held in His hand.
3. Paul stated that nothing, including future events (things to come), can separate us from Christ (Romans 8:38-39).
4. Paul and Jude stated that, once God started the process of presenting a person faultless

before God's throne, He would finish the job (Philippians 1:6; Jude 24).

5. Because Jesus, as our High Priest, can never die again, He will always be present to intercede for us when we sin (Hebrews 7:24-25). With Him as our Lawyer, we can never lose in God's courtroom (1 John 2:1).

6. The very fact that we become children of God when we receive Christ proves that we cannot lose our salvation (John 1:12, 13). My son may disobey me, but he can never undo his relationship with me. He will always be my son. Once an individual is born into God's family, he will always be a child of God. The fact that our new birth is described as an adoption further demonstrates our security (Romans 8:15; Galatians 4:5; Ephesians 1:5). In biblical times, a father might reject his natural-born son, but he could not legally separate himself from an adopted one.

7. We are sealed by the Holy Spirit the moment we believe, and that sealing remains secure until the day of redemption (Ephesians 1:13-14).

Salvation: Works versus Grace

The ultimate discussion is whether salvation is by grace apart from works or whether we have to help God accomplish the whole process. Let's find out God's opinion. After all, He wrote the book.

The Biblical Plan of Salvation

1. God is a holy God who will not accept sin or the individual who sins (Leviticus 19:2). He will punish that person in hell forever (Luke 16:23-26; Revelation 14:9-11)

2. Every person on earth has sinned, falling far short of God's holy standards (Romans 3:23; Psalm 14:2-3). No one could hope to spend eternity with God unless God did something to remove the sin barrier.

3. What God did was to send His Son, Jesus Christ, to die in our place and to be punished for our sins (John 3:16; Romans 5:8-10; 2 Corinthians 5:21).

4. Jesus did not stay dead but arose again, proving that He has the power to save others when they come to Him (1 Corinthians 15:3-4).

5. We must receive Jesus as our Savior in order to be with God. Receiving Jesus means that we must trust the resurrected Christ and Him alone to bring us into the presence of God (John 1:12; 14:6; Acts 4:12; Romans 10:13).

Salvation Is by Grace

The Bible teaches that salvation is by grace through the channel of our faith completely apart from works (Ephesians 2:8-9). Our righteousnesses (deeds done to be right with God) are as filthy rags in God's eyes (Isaiah 64:6). Religious deeds done to be accepted by God are worthless. We are made right with God not through the good deeds we do (Titus

3:5) but through God's mercy (i.e. God withholding what we deserve).

Grace and works are not to be put together in salvation (Romans 11:6). These two elements cannot be mixed. Either good works save us or God must. Throw religious pride out the window. Salvation is not a team effort or a combination of God and man succeeding together.

Biblical Position on the Law

Cults and false religions constantly misuse the word "law". They take the word "works" as used in the New Testament and try to make it apply to the Old Testament ceremonial law. This linguistic gymnastics will allow them to say that they do not believe in salvation by works; that is, they do not believe in the ceremonial law of the Old Testament. Then they turn right around and use James 2:26 (which we will discuss just a few lines down) and make works a part of salvation. In order to present the proper biblical position, we need to examine the use of the word "law" by the New Testament writers. An example is Romans 3, which deals with the law, not in ceremony, but as an instrument God used to teach mankind His holy standard. Paul demonstrates this use clearly in the chapter.

The purpose of God's righteous standard found in His moral law was to teach us we were sinners, not to bring us salvation (Romans 3:19-20). Because the law could not save us, we had to have a way to be right with God apart from the perfect life required by the law (Romans 3:21). The way to be right with God is through faith in Jesus Christ (Romans 3:22-26). The "law of faith" is not a new set of laws needed for salvation, but the simple fact that salvation is through faith in Christ Jesus (Romans 3:27-28). When we establish the law through our faith (Romans 3:31), we demonstrate the purpose of the law, which is not to save us, but to show us that we are sinners and that salvation must come from outside the law.

Working out Salvation

Philippians 2:12 teaches that we should *"work out your own salvation with fear and trembling."* In the next verse (v. 13 of chapter 2) we are again reminded that God is doing the work. Paul wrote in Ephesians 2:10, *"For we are His [God's] workmanship, created in Christ Jesus unto good works, which God hath before ordained that we should walk in them."* Interestingly, Paul wrote these words immediately after his strong declaration that salvation was by grace through faith. Our salvation is a wonderful reality accomplished by a holy God. He does the work of first saving and then changing our lives, making us into what He wants us to be. We are to have reverential respect ("fear and trembling") as we live our lives for others to see. But a child having respect for his parents is different than a child fearing a stranger who is trying to hurt him. Because of Jesus Christ, a believer never needs to be afraid of God's judgment, but he should always reverence and praise the God who redeemed him, the God who will accomplish His purpose in His children's lives.

Respect comes when we realize that God is serious about this business of making us into what He wants us to be. God in His perfect love for His people will not allow them to continue in sin without action on His part (Hebrews 12:6-11). God will discipline us in His love so that we will continue to become what He desires. We are His workmanship!

Chapter Two of James

This chapter is the cults' favorite passage! If you witness to religious people, you will at some time have to deal with this overused and misunderstood chapter. The verses that are quoted the most often from chapter two are verse 14, where James asks the question *"can faith save?"* in the negative, expecting a "no" answer, and verse 26 with its statement, *"faith without works is dead."* Oh, I almost forgot verse 21. It reads, *"Was not Abraham our father justified by works?"*

So what is James saying?

Faith is a vertical act witnessed by God resulting in the salvation of the individual. Works are horizontal and seen by men, and they testify that God is working in a person's life. The important concept we must remember then is that works demonstrate our faith before men as opposed to the cultic lie that works demonstrate our faith before God. This important concept is the point of what James is saying. The key phrase is in verse 24: *"Ye see."* Works relate to what man sees (Titus 3:8). Faith is what God sees (Hebrews 11:5-6). The big mistake comes when the cults make works a necessary part of what God sees for an individual to be saved. The biblical concept "works prove that an individual is saved" is true when the proving is before men, but not before God. God does not need proof; He sees the faith! Because men are unable to see faith, they must look at works.

James did not believe that one earns salvation, or he would not have written James 2:10: *"For whosoever shall keep the whole law, and yet offend in one point, he is guilty of all."* If a person sins only once in his entire life, he cannot reach God through works. One sin makes him guilty totally.

The phrase *"can faith save him?"* in James 2:14 of the King James Version could be translated to reflect the meaning of the verse more clearly with the implied word "that": *"can **that** faith save him?"* The whole first part of James 2 deals with being a Christian in more than word only. If one is a true believer in Christ, he will help the man who is hungry or has need. He will not do so because he is trying to be saved but because he is saved.

True faith results in works (James 2:18). When a person has been saved, he will perform good works as the natural result of God working in his life (Ephesians 2:10). The biblical logic is that good works are a result of salvation by faith in the true God. If a person claims to be saved but does not do good works, the faith he professes was never truly placed in Christ. Therefore, that kind of faith cannot save him.

James uses Abraham as an example. The biblical explanation of Abraham's justification before God appears in Romans 4:1-5. Abraham was saved because he exercised faith in God. This example brings us to an important point. Works fall far short of the sin they are trying to expiate; so a person trying to work his way to God grows deeper in debt to sin (Romans 4:5).

The biblical explanation of Abraham's justification before men (not just for his day, but for all time) is in James 2:21-24. Now get your Bible and follow this reasoning carefully. Verse 21 of James 2 is a fulfillment of verse 23. Verse 23 occurred before verse 21 (see Genesis 15:6 and Genesis 22). Therefore, Abraham had God's righteousness before the act of verse 21 (see v. 23). He had no need to be justified before God. He already was justified. His justification was before men when he offered up Isaac.

In a very real sense, God was using the whole incident to teach Abraham an important lesson: trust Me no matter what! When God used the phrase "now I know" in Genesis 22:12, He was saying those words for Abraham's benefit. Being God, He already knew the outcome of the lesson. God is amazingly patient as He instructs us!

James wrote chapter 2 to challenge believers not to play at being a Christian, but to live the truth of what God has done in their lives.

Eight

Demonic Doctrines

The Bible teaches that doctrines of demons will spread as we draw near the end of this age (1 Timothy 4:1). Paul cautions us that Satan can even appear as an angel of light (2 Corinthians 11:14). Paul further warns us that, if an angel appears and delivers a message that is contrary to the gospel of God's grace, that angel is a cursed being, and anyone listening to that being's message will experience a curse (Galatians 1:8-9). The issues are serious, and the demonic doctrines are a reality we all face in witnessing.

Baptism for the Dead

A Mormon doctrine teaches that Mormons need to be baptized for people who have already died. They believe that, when a non-Mormon dies, he goes to hell, which they call "spirit prison." They describe hell or spirit prison, however, as a classroom instead of a place of torment. (I realize that some students

I've met would draw no distinction between the two!) The whole doctrinal concept might be funny if the issues were not so serious. Anyway, according to Mormon doctrine, Mormons who have died and come down from paradise teach non-Mormons in spirit prison the truth of Mormonism. When a non-Mormon is ready to accept the truth of Mormonism, he's allowed to go up into paradise if someone here on earth has been baptized in a Mormon temple for him. Therefore, Mormons do much genealogical research by computer and other means. They check into their past, find their dead ancestors through extensive research, and get baptized for them, just in case the dead ancestor has accepted Mormonism in spirit prison and is waiting to ascend into paradise. Hence, this Mormon doctrine is a major work they do for their own personal salvation, a work that requires temples (special holy buildings that are different than their churches) to be built and genealogical research to be coordinated.

When one hears about a doctrine such as this one for the first time, a person tends to reject it because of its strange concepts. So we would be wise to remind ourselves again of a pertinent fact. The Mormon Church or any other cult or religion is not wrong because a doctrine it believes sounds strange or weird. These religious groups are wrong because their position disagrees with the Bible. Have I said those words before?

We have examined the Mormon doctrine, but what does the Bible teach?

Misunderstood Verses

1 Peter 3:18-20 and 4:6 are verses that Mormons use to "prove" that the dead are instructed in an eternal classroom setting. These verses, however, do not teach a second chance after death. Such a concept contradicts other Scriptures (Luke 16:26; Hebrews 9:27). The key to understanding these verses may rest in supplying the implied word "now" to the passages. The result in verse 19 of chapter 3 reads: *"Preached unto the spirits [who are now] in prison."* Christ preached by His Spirit through Noah to those who are now in the spiritual prison of hell, but Noah delivered the message while they were still alive here on earth. Verse 6 of chapter 4 would read: *"The gospel was preached also to them [who are now] dead."* The preaching occurred when they were alive. This position states that both passages refer to the gospel having been preached or proclaimed to people who rejected the message, died, and went to hell, where they are now. For example, let's pretend that I'm a waiter in a nice restaurant. As a waiter, I make this statement: "I told the people who are gone to pay the bill I left on their table." Obviously, they saw their bill and ran off before I could catch them, but as I did not insert the word "now", one might falsely conclude that I did not tell them to pay their bill until after they had gone. Here is the same message again: "As a waiter, I told people who are (now) gone to pay the bill I left on their table." To understand the Bible, one must examine a passage in light of what is normal, logical communication.

Many good scholars hold another position on the 1 Peter passages in several forms. The basic concept teaches that, between Christ's death and resurrection, His bodiless spirit went to the place where demonic spirits are bound and proclaimed His triumphal victory over them through His sacrifice for mankind. (Another possible version of this concept states that Christ most likely made this journey on the morning of His resurrection, but before He ascended to the Father (John 20:17).) The proclamation of the gospel that Jesus announced to the demonic horde of hell was that they had lost the battle to possess humanity, and they now faced God's ultimate judgment. In order to demonstrate the validity of this position, some of those who hold it point to the fact that active demons, who are not currently bound in such a prison, seem to be fearful of the potential judgment of being bound (Luke 8:31). Ultimately, the Scriptures indicate that all demons will suffer this type of eternal judgment (Matthew 25:41; Revelation 20:10).

Another verse that Mormons often quote usually stops most Christians in their tracks. They simply are not aware that such a verse in the Bible actually exists. **1 Corinthians 15:29** states, *"Else what shall they do which are baptized for the dead, if the dead rise not at all? Why are they then baptized for the dead?"* We have two main explanations for what Paul said here, as well as many other possible ideas which Bible scholars have presented through the centuries. We will focus briefly on the two main explanations. In either case, as we shall see in a moment, the rest of the Bible contradicts the Mormon interpretation that we should get baptized on behalf of and for dead people.

First is the real possibility that a cult in Paul's day was preaching the concept of baptism for the dead and that Paul alluded to its members and this practice to illustrate his point about the resurrection, even though he did not agree with them. (Compare his use of "we" and then his use of "they" in the chapter.) In other words, he was saying, "Even this group that is going around being baptized for dead people recognizes the importance of the resurrection, or they wouldn't be baptizing (even though it is for dead people). We know that they believe they will be resurrected because baptism pictures resurrection; they wouldn't put all that effort into baptizing for the dead if they didn't believe that the resurrection was going to happen."

A second possible explanation of the verse is that, when we are baptized, we witness to the fact that the dead will rise again (which is why we are placed down in the water and then elevated from it). We are baptized on behalf of the dead in that we show they will rise again.

Proper Biblical Teaching

What is the biblical opposition to the concept of baptism for the dead? The Bible is very straightforward on this issue with some uncompromising and very direct comments:

1. Temples are not for today (Acts 17:24; Matthew 27:51). Mormon doctrine teaches that you

must have a temple to perform this and other sacred ordinances, but temples are not part of God's program today.

2. We are not to do genealogical research from a theological position, especially for a theological purpose (1 Timothy 1:4; Titus 3:9).

3. Baptism does not save anyone (1 Corinthians 1:17; Acts 10:43). If it does not save a person, why do it for the dead, even if they had a second chance?

4. An impassable gulf lies between paradise and Hades (Luke 16:26). Even if one in hell would admit he was wrong, he has no way to get to paradise.

5. Judgment follows immediately after death (Hebrews 9:27) with no second chance.

Eternal Marriages

Some may wonder why I would think that the idea of being married forever is a demonic doctrine. Do I not love Beabea, my wife? Absolutely! A demonic doctrine does not have to be brutal or cruel or barbaric. All it has to be is deceiving. Any idea that causes a person to focus eternally on anything or anyone other than God is demonic. Husbands and wives have been given a precious gift of each other in this life, but it is a gift and it is from God. That gift must never become a substitute for God.

Mormons believe that a couple who is married in a Mormon temple by proper priesthood authority is married for time and eternity. They will exist together as husband and wife in both the spiritual and physical aspects of such a relationship throughout the eternal ages.

Biblical Position

First, the Bible clearly teaches that divine authority today does not rest with men, whether we are talking about a priesthood or prophets and apostles. Authority today rests in the Bible. The Bible teaches that Jesus' priesthood replaced all others (Hebrews 7:22-28; also see chapter on Biblical Authority.)

Secondly, Jesus stated that no marrying or giving in marriage occurs in heaven (Luke 20:27-36). The Mormon reply to this statement is that we do not marry in heaven. We marry on earth, and the marriage lasts through eternity. To make this reply is to ignore the entire context of the passage. Jesus was asked a question concerning a woman who had had seven husbands, all of whom died in their turns before she died. The question was: "To whom will she be married in heaven?" Then Jesus made His reply that the marriage relationship will not exist in heaven. The marriages were here on earth, and they would not extend to heaven. Despite Mormon doctrine, you cannot be married on earth and have that marriage continue in heaven.

For any disappointed couples who love their relationship very much, here is a word of encouragement. Although you will not be married in heaven, you will have a much closer relationship with your partner of this life (a perfect relationship); however, it will be the same relationship all believers enjoy together (John 17:23). The beauty of this promise is that it can begin to develop here on earth for brothers and sisters in Christ as well as for married couples, if they, too, know Christ.

Lost Tribes of Israel

British Israelism is a concept that both cult and non-cult individuals believe. Armstrongism is the most famous group that historically held this position. They once were considered one of the most difficult of the cults to reach. In recent years, they have undergone splits and major changes. The World Wide Church of God, the name of the main group, has returned to orthodox Christianity and apparently now teaches that salvation is solely by grace apart from works. If this change has truly happened, then God has done a marvelous work and a wonder!

Traditional British Israelism teaches that, after the fall of the northern kingdom of Israel, the ten tribes were scattered in the worldwide deportation. Eventually, Ephraim would become Britain and Manasseh the United States. This teaching is both historically and theologically wrong. Not only is it wrong, but it is a dangerous concept, removing true Jewish people from the center focus of God's purposes.

What is the proper biblical teaching?

Impossible Link

Ephraim and Manasseh are two tribes of people that are totally separate from each other. Historically, Manasseh did not come from Ephraim, but the United States did come from Britain. The United States cannot be Manasseh, and Britain cannot be Ephraim. Religious organizations have to spiritualize the relationship to make such claims.

No Lost Tribes

Biblically, no lost tribes exist. Ephraim and Manasseh were present in the land one hundred years after the Assyrian deportation (2 Chronicles 34:9). All twelve tribes were represented as present at the dedication of Zerubbabel's temple two hundred years after the Assyrian deportation (Ezra 6:17). Anna was of the tribe of Asher (Luke 2:36). Although people of each tribe were scattered during both deportations, they still retained their identity as the twelve tribes (James 1:1).

A Biblical Curse

Israel outside the land of Palestine is under a biblical curse until the day God brings them back to their land (Deuteronomy 28:63-68). Therefore, if the United States and Britain were Israel's descendants, they would not be receiving God's blessings. History teaches the opposite. Judgment on America may someday happen, but it will be because of sin, not because of a physical link to Jews who are not in their homeland.

Physical Jews Will Return to Israel

Both the northern and southern tribes will literally rejoin into one nation in the land of Palestine (Ezekiel 37:21-22). We probably saw the beginning of this melding in 1948 with the rebirth of Israel as a nation.

One Hundred and Forty-four Thousand

Jehovah's Witnesses teach that only one hundred forty-four thousand individuals from their group will be with Jehovah in heaven. Most Jehovah's Witnesses believe that those one hundred forty-four thousand have already been chosen and that the others will do well just to reach the future earth. The passage they use to demonstrate that Jehovah will select one hundred forty-four thousand people for heaven is Revelation 14:1-15.

Nature of the One Hundred Forty-four Thousand

What is the biblical nature of the one hundred forty-four thousand individuals from the book of Revelation? First, they are future. The only references to them in the Bible appear in Revelation 7 and 14. Anything described in chapters 6 to 22 of Revelation falls under the category of "the great day of His wrath" (Revelation 6:17), and present-day believers are promised deliverance from God's "wrath to come" (1 Thessalonians 1:10). Because we have not yet been delivered out of this world (Revelation 3:10 and 1 Thessalonians 4:15-17), we must conclude that Revelation 7 and 14 are still future.

Secondly, these passages describe the one hundred forty-four thousand. They are to be virgin males (Revelation 14:4) who are of the nation of Israel or the Jewish race (Revelation 7:4). None of these concepts matches the Jehovah's Witnesses' doctrine on this subject.

Not the Only Ones

What is very important (certainly to all of us) is that the one hundred forty-four thousand are not going to be the only ones in heaven with God. Praise the Lord; more than just one hundred forty-four thousand Israelites will be in heaven! The Bible teaches that people of every race will be there (Revelation 5:9). Further, a multitude no man can number will surround the throne of God (Revelation 7:9-17).

Preexistence

Different religious groups hold varied ideas of preexistence, but in this section, we will deal with the Mormon concept. Mormonism teaches that we all existed in a spiritual preexistence, born to "Mrs. God" before we were born on this earth. This concept is not to be confused with reincarnation, which will be addressed later. Mormonism also teaches that some of the spirit children, of whom we were all a part, did good deeds in the preexistence, and some did bad deeds. All of this prior history is supposed to affect how we are born on earth.

What does the Bible teach on this subject?

Misunderstood Verses

God declares in **Job 38:4-7**, *"Where wast thou when I laid the foundations of the earth...and all the sons of God shouted for joy?"* The Mormons claim that the "sons of God" referenced here are spirit children born in the preexistence who will later be born as humans on earth. They also state that God's question implied that Job was present before the foundation of the world. The context teaches otherwise. The question God asked Job was a negative question, implying that Job was not present in creation; therefore, Job's opinion had to take second place to God's. Job 38:21 finds God pointing out to Job that he really did not know anything about creation because he wasn't around at the time or, literally, not yet born.

The use of the word "sons" here does not have to carry the meaning of literal birth, and the passage gives us no reason to believe that it does. The Man Christ Jesus is the only One to be uniquely born of the Father through the Holy Spirit in the virgin birth, and then only in the sense that the Holy Spirit prepared a body in the womb of Mary for God the Son to indwell (John 3:16; Luke 1:35; Hebrews 10:5). Therefore, the use of the word "sons" in Job indicates identification of created beings with the God who created them, not preexistent children. We have no doubt that an angelic race separate from man did exist at the creation, but we must note two important points about them:

1. Angels are not to be linked with mankind; they are separate (Psalm 8:4-5).
2. Angels are created beings, not born into existence (Ezekiel 28:14-15).

In **Jeremiah 1:5,** we read God's statement concerning his prophet, Jeremiah: *"Before I formed* *thee in the belly I knew thee."* Mormons use this verse to try to prove that Jeremiah existed before he was conceived in his mother's womb. This verse is a simple declaration of the foreknowledge of God, and nothing else (Isaiah 46:9-10).

John 9:2: *"And His disciples asked Him, saying, Master, who did sin, this man, or his parents, that he was born blind?"* Mormons make the claim that the disciples were aware of a preexistence doctrine or they would not have implied that a man could be born blind for his sin. According to the Mormons, the sin had to occur in preexistence before the blind man was born. Again, the answer is the foreknowledge of God. Nothing here implies that the disciples believed in preexistence, but as they were aware of the many Old Testament passages that taught God's foreknowledge, they believed that God could know a person's life ahead of time.

Biblical Opposition to Preexistence

Jesus is the only Man who has come from a preexistence (John 3:13). He is the only One who could ascend to heaven on His own power. Further, Paul taught that physical life comes first, then the spiritual, not the reverse (1 Corinthians 15:46). When Romans 9:11 refers to *"the children being not yet born, neither having done any good or evil"*, it clarifies the point that actions of good or evil are not possible before birth. Therefore, we could not have existed in a preexistence as the Mormons teach, doing either good or bad deeds.

Reincarnation

The concept of reincarnation is so alien to the Bible that the cults who believe it will rarely use the Bible to attempt to prove their position. Mainly, non-Bible cults hold this position (although some groups today who claim to believe the Bible are now embracing the concept). Reincarnation in its basic form teaches that all life is evolving, seeking a state of less suffering and moving to the point of no suffering. One's actions in this life determine the level of the next life when we are reborn on this earth. Ultimately, a form of final oblivion may be achieved, which breaks the endless circle of the life's movement upward, and then peace comes. Hence, the concept of achieving peace within oneself is of great importance. This concept of recycling life has opened the door for the transcendental meditation movement. (Meditation is not anti-biblical, but it is to be focused in Christ, who He is, and what He has done to and for us.)

The use of Bible verses in dealing with reincarnation will probably not bring immediate results with people who do not accept the Bible as an authority. We do not, however, apologize for the Bible. For us to know what the Bible teaches on reincarnation is very important, just as we should for any subject, but the most profitable approach may rest in sharing the peace that God gives in salvation and the comfort true believers receive in their daily lives as we focus on Christ. God's Word promises peace in salvation (Romans 5:1-2) and peace in the Christian life (John 14:27; 16:33; Philippians 4:7; Colossians 3:15; 2

Thessalonians 3:16). This peace is not based on emotion, spiritual attainment, or personal achievement, but on truth. We can trust the promises of God!

Biblical Opposition to Reincarnation
1. People can only die once physically, not over and over again as they move through levels of existence (Hebrews 9:27).
2. In the story of the rich man and Lazarus, we are instructed that no way back to this life exists (Luke 16:19-31).
   (Biblical exceptions to the above points include the people Christ raised from the dead as well as the fact that we all will be resurrected someday. The important point to note is that none of the exceptions fit into any kind of concept found in reincarnation.)
3. The fact that Jacob and Esau had done neither good nor evil before their births would remove the possibility of their living on this earth previously and progressing to the next life based on their actions (Romans 9:11).

Soul Sleep: Eternity versus Annihilation
Jehovah's Witnesses, among other cults (and some evangelical Christians), deny the doctrine that eternal punishment lasts forever in hell. Instead, some religious groups teach only annihilation for the lost who, as they claim, will be cast into hell and be burned up. Others teach that the ungodly will never wake from their eternal sleep. This concept is consis-

tent with the idea that when people die, they do not go to heaven or hell. Instead, the soul supposedly sleeps in the grave.

Jehovah's Witnesses claim that the Hebrew word *Sheol* and the Greek word *Hades* mean only "grave." We can agree with them in the sense that these two words are translations of each other between two languages and, therefore, carry basically the same meaning. An example would be Psalm 16:10 where the English word "hell" is a translation of the Hebrew word *Sheol*. When the New Testament quotes this passage, the Greek word used is *Hades* (Acts 2:27). We cannot agree, however, that the two words mean "grave."

In Greek mythology, *Hades* was the unseen world, and all the dead went there. It was not a place where people ceased to exist. As the Greek-speaking world spread and a need for a Greek translation of the Old Testament (the Septuagint) arose, the word *Hades* was selected as the translation of the word *Sheol*. The translators could not have thought that the word *Sheol* meant only the grave, because they used the Greek word *Hades,* which described a living existence after death.

The King James Bible translators' solution to the wide use of the word *Sheol* in somewhat vague passages in the Old Testament was to translate it "grave" or "hell," based on the context of the passage. This solution was understandable, but it has caused considerable unforeseen confusion. To try to choose what a word means by context involves some inter-pretation during translation. Context certainly helps us understand what a word means in any passage, but one must start with the actual meaning of a word and then use context to clarify it. Perhaps the best single translation of the word with the least amount of interpretation is the phrase "the place of the dead." Let's look at some of the passages that Jehovah's Witnesses and others have misunderstood.

Misunderstood Verses

Psalm 6:5: *"For in death there is no remembrance of thee: in the grave who shall give thee thanks?"* The Hebrew word is *Sheol* (the place of the dead). This verse means that the dead do not remember or give thanks with the physical tongue where other men might hear and benefit. It does not mean that we will not be able to worship God in thanksgiving and praise after death.

Psalm 31:17: *"Let me not be ashamed, O LORD; for I have called upon thee: let the wicked be ashamed, and let them be silent in the grave."* Again the Hebrew word is *Sheol* (the place of the dead). The wicked are silent physically in death. They are also unable to send communication from the place of the dead (Luke 16:27-31).

Ecclesiastes 9:10: *"Whatsoever thy hand findeth to do, do it with thy might; for there is no work, nor device, nor knowledge, nor wisdom, in the grave, whither thou goest."* The Hebrew word again is *Sheol* (place of the dead). The fact that anyone uses the book of Ecclesiastes to build a doctrine demonstrates his lack of understanding as to why the book was recognized as Scripture. God put Ecclesiastes in the canon of Scripture to reveal the way the natural man thinks (note key phrases "under the sun," "I perceive," "I said in my heart," found in Ecclesiastes 1:9, 17; 2:1). Ecclesiastes 9:10 shares a humanist's depressed philosophy of life. The natural man sees death as an end to all things (Ecclesiastes 6:6).

Isaiah 38:18: *"For the grave cannot praise thee, death can not celebrate thee: they that go down into the pit cannot hope for thy truth."* Once more the Hebrew word is *Sheol* (place of the dead). The same simple explanation given earlier for Psalm 6:5 is the answer to the Jehovah's Witnesses' position on this passage. Death limits the physical body's ability to speak forth praise.

1 Thessalonians 4:13: *"But I would not have you to be ignorant, brethren, concerning them which are asleep, that ye sorrow not, even as others which have no hope."* Again, the verse must refer to the physical body because of the biblical teaching of conscious life after death (Luke 16:19-31). If this reference (1 Thessalonians 4:13) were the only passage concerning death, one might come to the same conclusion as some of the cults. The Bible, however, has many passages that demonstrate the conscious existence of life immediately after death, and they must be taken into account. Let's look at some of them.

Proper Biblical Teaching on Life after Death

1. The place of the dead (*Sheol*) is a place of consciousness. Those who are in hell hold conversations (Isaiah 14:9-10; Ezekiel 32:21).

Jonah compares his conscious time within the great fish as being in hell itself (Jonah 2:2).

2. Jesus said that we are to fear God, who can both kill and then cast into hell (Luke 12:5). Jesus refers to two distinct occurrences here: death and hell.

3. Jesus told the thief on the cross that he would be with Jesus in paradise on the same day as his death (Luke 23:42-43). Some cults (Jehovah's Witnesses mostly) try to make the word "today" link with the phrase, "I say unto thee," so that the complete statement would be, "I say unto thee today, you shall be with me in paradise." Jehovah's Witnesses' *New World Translation* takes this approach. By doing so, they make Jesus' promise happen today instead of His promise being kept today. Otherwise, the thief and Jesus both have immediate life after death. To make this kind of punctuation change in translation ignores the context and how good Greek scholars have translated this passage throughout the centuries. The importance of the context appears in the fact that Jesus is responding to the thief's desire to be in Christ's kingdom one day. Christ's answer to the thief is that he will not have to wait; today he will be in paradise.

4. James 2:26 teaches that the body without the spirit is dead, and 2 Corinthians 5:8 teaches that to be absent from the body is to be present with the Lord. (Of course, this promise refers to the saved individual.)

5. The martyred people of Revelation 6:9-11 are conscious around the throne of God.

6. The story of the rich man and Lazarus describes in exact detail the events following death (Luke 16:19-31). Jehovah's Witnesses claim that this passage is a parable and is symbolic. Their conclusion is wrong for the following reasons. This story is not a general story, but one that involves a certain rich man and a certain beggar named Lazarus. Although a parable may have a real setting that occurs in everyday life, parables are not about actual people, and the characters in this story are identified as actual people. (Even if this story were a parable, a parable is based on commonly understood facts known to people of the area. Parables are also based on true realities that are familiar to the people. Those that listened would be able to relate to the accepted concepts of Abraham's bosom and hell.) Also, if these places were symbols, then those who label them so would have to face the truth that the reality of a symbol is always much worse than the symbol representing it. Finally, if this story is not true, then Jesus lied and purposely misrepresented what life after death is really like.

7. In a very serious passage found in Mark 9:42-48, Jesus taught clearly that an individual cast into everlasting hell does not simply burn up in a place that exists forever. (Some religious groups teach that hell will last forever, but not the people who are cast into it.) Instead, hell

is a place where the fire is not quenched (see Revelation 14:9-11). Certain cults as well as a few somewhat "unorthodox theologians" use such passages as 2 Thessalonians 1:9, which speak of everlasting destruction, to support their view of nonexistence after death. The important point to notice is that the process of destruction is everlasting. A person cannot exist in everlasting destruction unless he is forever being destroyed. He cannot simply burn up and cease to exist. This thought is very sobering, and it emphasizes the burden we need to have for the dear people of the cults and false religions of the world.

Nine

Practical Responses

Temporary Alternative to Discussion

We would be foolish to believe that every Christian is ready to meet cult members in a one-on-one discussion. This reality does not remove the responsibility of every Christian to prepare to witness. Yet, what do you do until you are prepared? You do not want to be unfriendly and ruin the chances of another Christian to witness later on, but sometimes people from the cults are so forward that they put you in a position of either discussing both parties' beliefs or closing the door. What can you do?

Here is a temporary solution until you are ready for a full discussion. Tell your visitors that you are very happy they dropped by. You love the Lord Jesus very much, but at the present moment you are unable to talk with them. Have a tract available or some other good Christian material that does not attack their organization or make them look stupid. Then ask for their phone number or email address. The phone number does not have to be a personal number if they are hesitant to give one. It can be their organizational headquarters or somewhere with access to an answering machine. The advantage in using email is that it is a great way to keep in contact, and email gives you time to research your answers. If you ask for a way to communicate with them, they will probably not feel that they have to start a conversation at that moment. They are likely not to pressure you in the hope of another visit. You will also then have a contact for the time when you feel ready to talk with them. This approach keeps the opportunity open.

Of course, immediately begin preparing yourself for the future conversation. If you don't contact them, they probably will come back!

Proper Use of Anti-Cult Material

As we have already stated in the previous section and in the chapter on attitude, one has to be careful of the literature he distributes. Tracts and other materials that deal directly with a cult, mentioning the name of the cult and its founder, especially in a negative way, often do more harm than good if given during the initial contact.

This material has a proper use. If a person of the cults has come to the point where he sees that what he has been taught disagrees with the Bible and he wants to do some research, then the material can be quite effective. Another way to use it is if someone is starting to lean toward joining a cult and also wants some research material. Again, the important point in each case is that the Bible disagrees with the cult. The Bible must still remain the focus.

Some Christian groups or organizations seem to produce an attack attitude against cults, intentionally or not. Our attitude toward people in this kind of group should be as Jesus said in Mark 9:38-40. They are not our enemies. They are brothers and sisters in Christ who have a different approach than we do concerning the winning of cult members to our Savior. We do not have to use their approach, but we can pray for them, that God will use them and the material they give to cult members.

This book is designed to help you, the reader, witness to cults, but it can only be the beginning of your preparation. With this book or any other material, knowing the Bible is the real key to reaching the people of the cults for Christ.

Suggested Visitation Passages

Basically, up to this point, we have dealt with what to do if the cults come to your home. What do you do when you knock on the door of a cult member while you are on visitation? What about talking to a cult member at work or sitting on a plane? Actually, most of what we have already shared applies to a visitation call or any general friendly witnessing. However, there are differences.

First, you must usually initiate the discussion. As in any conversation with a cult or religious individual, you will want to make truth the focal point of the discussion and begin to establish the authority of the Bible. Be careful to define your terms and concentrate on the issue of salvation. You must remember, however, if you are the guest or you are in a neutral area such as a park or other public location, that you will not be able to establish rules of conversation as easily as when the discussion is in your home.

Secondly, in most cases the members of a religious group you meet casually or in door-to-door visitation will not be nearly as difficult to handle as those who come to your door. You may, however, be surprised on occasion; so always expect a challenge! (Just about the time you begin to believe that you are capable of dealing with cult individuals effectively, God will send you someone that will cause you to need your Lord's guidance more then ever.) Always be courteous to anyone with whom you are talking about Christ, whether the other person is from a cult or not. People are only human; so do not push them in the discussion any more than you would want to be pushed if you were in their position.

When you begin a conversation, you must decide if you should refer to Scripture right away or if you should develop the relationship before bringing in the Bible. Don't make the mistake of never getting to the Bible. God's Word gives life, and you cannot bring spiritual resurrection without it. Now, the important question is what passages you should use to open the conversation and make the contact. Quite a few passages are good, such as **Acts 16:25-34** and **John 3:1-18**. (John 3 is a good passage, because Jesus is dealing with a religious man, but anyone using this passage needs to be prepared to answer the cult's argument that John 3:5 deals with baptism.)

Perhaps one of the best passages to use with a cult or religious individual who is open in some fashion to the Bible is **2 Timothy 3:15-16**. Verse 15 teaches that the biblical way of salvation is through faith in Jesus Christ. Verse 16 teaches that the Bible (Scripture) gives us all we need to know about God and how to be right with Him. This passage will help you establish the authority of the Bible and will also open up the conversation to the way of salvation.

A concluding passage of Scripture as the conversation closes is **1 John 5:9-13**. We have already discussed the use of this passage under the chapter "Priority Goal."

Bible As Far As Translated Correctly

What do you do when a Mormon rejects what you are sharing from Scripture and makes the statement that the Bible is God's Word but only as far as translated correctly? His implication is that the verse you have shared with him is probably not accurate, even though he may not have been that direct in his comment. What does he mean? He probably does not mean that the verse was incorrectly translated, despite the fact that he used those words. Most likely he means that the Bible developed errors as manuscripts were copied through the centuries. You should, however, take the comment as shared and proceed. You must remember that the phrase "as far as translated correctly" grants authority and excuse to the individual who uses it to accept or reject the Bible where he wants.

In responding to the accurate translation of the Bible issue, here are some legitimate questions to ask.

1. Ask the Mormon, "Are you certain that this particular verse under discussion is translated incorrectly?" This question is important, for it forces the Mormon to make an exact statement concerning the verse under discussion instead of a general remark that the Bible is the Word of God only as far as it is translated correctly. The Mormon must face and accept or directly reject teachings of the specific verse as inaccurate. He should not sidestep the issue.

2. If the Mormon claims that the verse under discussion is not translated correctly, then ask him, "What parts of the Bible are translated correctly, and what parts are not?" Politely follow this question with permission to ask another very honest question: "Do you only accept the verses that you feel agree with you?" No one, including we who are sharing Christ, has the option of accepting only the parts of the Bible he likes.

3. Many verses teach that the Bible cannot become a book of error (e.g. 1 Peter 1:23). Ask the Mormon individual, "Are all those verses translated incorrectly?" The issue is simple. Are all the verses such as 1 Peter 1:23 that teach that the Word of God cannot become corrupt, corrupt themselves? If the Bible could have errors, then most certainly 1 Peter 1:23

has a major error, for it teaches that the Bible cannot have errors!

Point of No Discussion

At some point, continuing a conversation with a person of the cults may no longer be constructive. This point can come early in a conversation, but it usually comes toward the end, if at all. The point of no discussion arrives when the cult person absolutely rejects biblical authority and chooses his religion's teachings over the Bible. Once a person rejects God's Word, Christians have very little left to share, for all we know about God is within the Bible's pages. We are not talking about a conversation with a member of a cult that does not hold the Bible as Scripture. In that case, use the concepts discussed in the chapter "Friendly Discussions" about non-Bible cults to initiate the conversation. We are talking about the moment when the cult person, no matter the background, understands what the Bible says and rejects it for his cult teachings. Do we give up? Never! We are simply backing off and giving the Holy Spirit time to work. Always continue to build your relationship with this person who still needs Christ!

When in a conversation where you find yourself at the point of no further discussion, share honestly with the individual why the conversation cannot continue: he has chosen his religion over the Bible. This concept may immediately concern him. Accepting that he is actually rejecting the Bible may be difficult for him. If the cult individual cannot agree with your statement and still believes that the Bible does teach his position, then you have not yet arrived at the point of no discussion; continue talking with him. If he agrees with your statement, you may be at the point of no discussion. Tell him that you love him in Christ, and let the conversation end. If it does not, a door may still be open, however small, and we should not close it totally until God does. As long as someone wants to continue to discuss God, we must seek the Lord for the patience to continue to talk with him or her.

Ephesians 2:8-9 and the Mormons

Christians can use Ephesians 2:8-9 in a special way with Mormons. This approach is quite effective in most cases, but we must remember that each Mormon may have his own way of explaining his doctrine. Therefore, when one uses this approach, he must be prepared to adapt it to each individual with whom he speaks.

Mormons have basically two different salvations within their system of doctrine. The first salvation is "resurrection." It is by God's grace because (according to Mormon doctrine) Christ paid for Adam's sin, thereby providing resurrection and making it a free gift to all mankind. An important point to remember is that the first salvation (resurrection) is for everyone. The second salvation is called "exaltation." Exaltation, according to Mormonism, results in godhood and the presence of God. Good Mormons receive it because of the worthiness of each individual, demonstrated by his good works through obedience to the Mormon gospel. Christ's atonement is involved with this concept, but it only becomes effective as the Mormon proves his worthiness through his good works.

The direct biblical opposition to these false doctrines is in Ephesians 2:8-9. Verse 8 with its phrase "through faith" contradicts the Mormons' first salvation concept that resurrection is a gift to everyone. Verse 9 with its phrase "not of works" contradicts the Mormons' second salvation concept that he can earn exaltation (an extended form of high salvation) through good works. [13]

We have asked Mr. Christian from chapter four to assist us again in a pretend demonstration of witnessing. This example is only an illustration. The real thing involves real people, and nothing is pretend about that. Remember, not every conversation will be this complicated, but being ready always helps. Note also that many Mormons with whom you talk may not be as open as the one in our illustration, and working through each point in your conversation may take longer than this example does.

MR. CHRISTIAN: Would you explain to me how you believe an individual receives salvation into the presence of God?

MR. MORMON: We believe salvation comes through faith and obedience to the gospel of Jesus Christ.

MR. CHRISTIAN: You used the word "obedience". What does that involve?

MR. MORMON: The gospel in its basic form is faith in Christ, repentance, baptism for the forgiveness of sins, and the laying on of hands for the gift of the Holy Ghost.

MR. CHRISTIAN: Do you have other things you must do?

MR. MORMON: Yes, temple work and mission work would be a part.

MR. CHRISTIAN: Then you believe that salvation comes through the performance of good works?

MR. MORMON: Good works are certainly a part, but I don't know if I would say good works save us. The *Book of Mormon* teaches that we are saved by faith after all we can do.

MR. CHRISTIAN: According to what you just said, you must work as hard as you can to qualify for the right to have faith save you. Does that belief not make works necessary for salvation?

MR. MORMON: Well, yes, it would. James 2 says that faith without works is dead.

MR. CHRISTIAN: The difference in the way you see that verse and the way I see it is that you believe faith is insufficient without works. I

	believe that works are a result of true faith.
MR. MORMON:	Then the disagreement is a case of your opinion versus my opinion.
MR. CHRISTIAN:	I could understand your position if James 2 were the only passage dealing with the subject. Romans 11:6 informs us that you cannot mix grace and works, and Ephesians 2:8 says, "For by grace are ye saved." If I may ask, what does the Bible mean when it says we are saved by grace?
MR. MORMON:	We believe that more than one type of salvation exists. Probably what is being spoken of here is resurrection.
MR. CHRISTIAN:	Do you believe that everyone will be resurrected?
MR. MORMON:	Yes.
MR. CHRISTIAN:	Then what do you do with the next phrase "through faith"? The verse says, "For by grace are ye saved through faith." Will only those who have faith be resurrected?
MR. MORMON:	No, everyone will be resurrected.
MR. CHRISTIAN:	What do you do with the verse?

MR. MORMON: I'm not sure. Perhaps I was mistaken. Maybe this verse refers to exaltation. Faith is the first step in exaltation.

MR. CHRISTIAN: What is exaltation?

MR. MORMON: Exaltation is the highest level of salvation that can be received. It gives us the very presence of God.

MR. CHRISTIAN: Does exaltation lead to godhood?

MR. MORMON: Possibly, but that is not our focus. Honoring God the Father and His Son, Jesus Christ, through strengthening the family is what Latter-day Saints are all about.

MR. CHRISTIAN: You said that faith was the first step in exaltation. Are there other steps?

MR. MORMON: Well, yes.

MR. CHRISTIAN: What are they?

MR. MORMON: I've already mentioned them: repentance, baptism, receiving the Holy Ghost, and so on.

MR. CHRISTIAN: Then exaltation is the salvation we mentioned already, which is received through faith and by doing the works the Mormon Church says to do.

MR. MORMON: Yes, that is correct.

MR. CHRISTIAN:	Ephesians 2:8-9 reads, "For by grace are ye saved through faith; and that not of yourselves: it is the gift of God: not by works, lest any man should boast." The last part of these verses contradicts your second salvation, known as exaltation, because the salvation the Bible specifies here is "not of works." No matter which salvation you choose, these verses in Ephesians 2 contradict your choice.
MR. MORMON:	I said earlier that works do not save us. Faith saves us. We do the works to demonstrate our faith.
MR. CHRISTIAN:	Is faith all you need for salvation?
MR. MORMON:	No, you need to prove your faith by doing other things.
MR. CHRISTIAN:	Then works are necessary?
MR. MORMON:	Yes, but faith is still what saves us.
MR. CHRISTIAN:	How do you receive forgiveness of sins: by faith alone?
MR. MORMON:	No, by baptism.
MR. CHRISTIAN:	How do you receive the Holy Ghost: by faith alone?
MR. MORMON:	No, through the laying on of hands.

MR. CHRISTIAN: You shared earlier that you believe you can be exalted, perhaps become a god. How do you become exalted: by faith alone?

MR. MORMON: No, through obedience to the laws and ordinances of the gospel of Christ.

MR. CHRISTIAN: Are forgiveness of sins, receiving the Holy Ghost, and exaltation, part of salvation?

MR. MORMON: Yes.

MR. CHRISTIAN: I don't understand. You say that all of these things are part of salvation, and you say that faith saves you, but faith does not accomplish the things I just listed. What exactly does faith accomplish?

MR. MORMON: It is the most important thing. It gives meaning to everything we do.

MR. CHRISTIAN: But faith alone cannot save?

MR. MORMON: That is correct.

MR. CHRISTIAN: Ephesians 2:8-9 says we are saved by grace through faith apart from works. I believe that you must decide between the Mormon doctrine of salvation, which is faith plus works, and what the Bible says in Ephesians 2:8-9, which is salvation by faith alone. The Bible leaves no in-between option.

John 1:1 and the Jehovah's Witnesses

Without much difficulty, Christians can show the Word mentioned in John 1:1 to be Jesus Christ. John 1:14 teaches that the Word was made flesh and is the only begotten of the Father. Hence, we know that the Word is Jesus. Therefore, John 1:1 clearly teaches that Jesus (the Word) is God. It reads, *"In the beginning was the Word, and the Word was with God, and the Word was God."* Here the Jehovah's Witnesses step in and say that this translation of the Greek is not correct. In their New World Translation, they translate the last phrase "and the Word was a god." They claim that they are following a basic Greek rule, which does exist. The rule is that when a noun lacks the definite article, it is not to be translated with the article "the "; instead, it is to be translated with the article, "a." The word *Theos* (God, in this case) does lack the definite article; so their translation is "a god." Nevertheless, their translation is incorrect.

Now, let's re-examine the issues closely and thoroughly. Although virtually every major English Bible translates John 1:1c, "the Word was God", the Jehovah's Witness New World Translation translates the clause, "the Word was a god." Again, the Jehovah's Witness argues that, because the original Greek has no definite article with the predicate nominative *Theos* (God), the noun should be translated as an indefinite noun, i.e., "a god."

The New World Translation of John 1:1, however, is erroneous. It flounders on the fact that to translate *Theos* in John 1:1c as "a god" ignores another rule in Greek grammar that a predicate nominative noun without the article that occurs prior to the linking verb (which is the construction in John 1:1c) is rarely, if ever, indefinite but is usually qualitative in meaning. A qualitative noun emphasizes the nature or essence of the thing described. In the case of John 1:1, the idea conveyed is that the Word was God, i.e., of the same nature as the Father.

Among the many examples of this same construction in John's writings are the following: John 1:14 ("the Word became flesh", not "a flesh"); 1 John 1:5 ("God is light", not "a light"); and 1 John 4:8 ("God is love", not "a love"). In each instance, one can clearly see the emphasis on the nature of the thing described as well as the inappropriateness of translating each term as an indefinite noun.

We should also note that the New World Translation is largely inconsistent in applying its rule that the term *Theos* without the definite article should be considered indefinite. In the Greek New Testament are some two hundred eighty-two occurrences of *Theos* without the article. At sixteen places, the New World Translation has either "a god", "god", "gods", or "godly". Sixteen out of two hundred eighty-two means that the translators were faithful to their translation principle only six percent of the time.

A glance at the Greek of John 1:1-18 furnishes a revealing example of this inconsistency. *Theos* occurs eight times (vv. 1b, 1c, 2, 6, 12, 13, 18a, and 18b) and has the definite article only twice (vv. 1b and 2). Yet the New World Translation translates *Theos* six times as "God," once as "a god," and once as "the god." This inconsistency leads one to conclude that the Jehovah's Witness translation of John 1:1c as "a god" is a matter of theological bias against the deity of Christ rather than loyalty to a supposed grammatical principle. [14]

True Bible students have no choice. The translation must be "the Word was God," not "the Word was a god." For the record, the definite article is used in John 20:28 by Thomas in recognition of the deity of the risen Christ. He said to Christ (literally translated), "The Lord of me, and *the* God of me" (emphasis mine). Jesus did not rebuke him for his statement but accepted his worship. Finally, another problem for the Jehovah's Witnesses is that insisting that this translation should be "a god" would mean Jesus was a second god, and that idea would contradict their theology that only one God exists.

Prophecy and the Cults

Almost all Bible cults use prophecy as a major part of their belief system. The reason for this practice is credibility and validation. Understanding why the decision is made to do so in the early days of a cult's development is easy. Much of Bible prophecy is written in abstract concepts mixed with multiple visions. Even orthodox denominations disagree in a major way on what most passages mean. This disagreement leaves a wide-open door for personal interpretation by each cult.

Angels and Visions

An excellent example of this wide-open door is in Revelation 14:6-7, where an angel flies through heaven with a gospel message to share with the world. Claiming that the prophesied angel appeared to a particular religious leader to commission him or her to help with the task would be a very easy step. This claim would give that leader divine authority from heaven. Reaching people of that organization would be very difficult, as its members would see themselves as sent by God's angel. (Incidentally, Mormons believe that this heavenly angel is Moroni who delivered the *Book of Mormon* to Joseph Smith.)

Such a claim has to be faced head-on. Probably one of the best questions to ask immediately is: where in the religion's records is the record that their angel said the exact words that the angel in the Bible said? God's visions are exact, and they must be fulfilled exactly. Secondly, did the angel appearing to the religious leader teach anything contrary to biblical grace? (See Galatians 1:6-9). If so, then maybe the angel fits the 2 Corinthians 11:13-15 warning instead of the Revelation angel.

Religion Out of Control

A second reason the cults enjoy manipulating prophetic Scripture is the end result of creating religious fervor. The old "end of the world" syndrome motivates people to sell homes, forsake jobs, donate all their money, leave family and friends, and even surrender their will completely. Humans desire the supernatural to break through in their everyday existence. People are looking for something, anything, to give meaning to life or to rescue them from having to live on this planet for the rest of their existence without purpose. The Bible describes mankind's battle against emptiness in 2 Timothy 3:1-9. Unless we, who know the solution (relationship with God), share that solution with others, the cults will continue to attract desperate, searching people.

Book of Acts

The Bible books most often quoted by cults are probably the prophetic books of Ezekiel, Daniel, and Revelation, plus the book of Acts. Obviously, any of the major or minor prophet books would be popular because of their visions, but why the book of Acts? The reason for the many quotes taken from Acts is that it is transitional in nature. It takes God's people from the old system of God's working through the law to a new system of grace. The Gospel accounts take place during the time of the law, even though Christ is introducing the concepts that are the basis of the rest of the New Testament. The first ten chapters of Acts are a step-by-step account of God's expanding the outreach of believing Jews to the part-Jewish Samaritans and finally to the Gentiles. Along the way, God uses signs to convince the Jewish people this expansion was happening. Even Peter had difficulty understanding what God was doing. He fully expected the great tribulation soon after he preached at Pentecost (Acts 2:16-20). Had the nation of Israel responded to the message that Jesus was their Messiah, Peter would have been right. Before one can understand what is happening in Acts, one needs to understand this transition process.

An excellent example of the transitional nature of Acts occurs in chapter 19, verses 1-7. Read the story and ask yourself this question. In any other time in history, could truly saved believers in God (disciples of John the Baptist who left the Middle East for Asia Minor before Jesus came on the scene) have lived without knowledge of Christ after His resurrection and the coming of His Spirit? This unique period would never occur again. How easy building incorrect doctrine based on Acts 19:1-7 would be if an individual did not understand the transitional nature of the book of Acts! A believer receives the Holy Spirit when he trusts in Christ, and here were a group of believers who had never trusted in Christ. The situation occurs only here, and God leads Paul to a special way of bringing the Holy Spirit into their group by the laying on of hands. Each time in Acts when a people group receives the Holy Spirit (the Jews in Acts 2:1-4; the Samaritans in Acts 8:14-17), God does something special to help the Jewish people understand the expanding work of God. Finally in Acts 10:44-47, He opens the gospel door to the Gentiles, and the pattern is set to receive the Holy Spirit when one believes. Acts 19 deals with the last people group (believers baptized under John the Baptist's ministry who did not know of Christ). To take Acts 19:1-7 and apply it to the way God is working today would be wrong.

Book of Revelation

Getting drawn into a major discussion about the meaning of a multitude of verses in this last prophetic book of the Bible would be really easy. That tendency should be avoided. The real issue again in witnessing to religious people is salvation, but having a basic understanding of the makeup of the book of Revelation will be helpful. Let's look at a breakdown of the chapters.

Chapters 1-3 of Revelation deal with churches in existence toward the end of the life of John the Apostle. Chapters 4-5 show us the throne room of God. The dispensational view is that this room is heaven immediately after the rapture (catching up) of church-age believers. Chapters 6-19 are generally recognized as the tribulation period, and therefore are future events. Most cults, some religious groups, and some evangelical Christians, however, view these events as happening in the past, now, just recently, or very soon. In response to their view, Revelation 6:17 identifies this section as the great day of God's wrath. The indication is that these events are still future. Next, a literal interpretation of chapter 20 promotes only one conclusion: this passage describes the millennial reign of Christ (one thousand years). Finally, chapters 21-22 describe eternity.

Future Prophets

Without question, the book of Revelation has prophets in what is a future setting. The Bible makes clear that Scripture is complete (John 16:13). Christians have no need for additional doctrinal revelations. Hence, the logical conclusion is that the future Revelation prophets will be speaking directionally to Israel under divine guidance, not revealing any new doctrine. To comprehend this concept, we need to realize that the book of Revelation describes a future time when God is moving to bring the earth back into direct submission to Him. Dispensational study indicates that the tribulation time of Revelation chapters 6-19 completes the ancient prophecy of Daniel found in 9:24-27. This view gives the book of Revelation an Old Testament Jewish setting, as God brings His chosen people of Israel back to Himself.

Restitution of All Things

Mormons teach that the reference in Acts 3:20-21 about God restoring all things came to pass through their founder, Joseph Smith, as God supposedly gave back to him all that had been lost through the centuries. A close examination of the verses reveals that the restitution of all things in Acts 3:21 is exactly that and therefore this passage must apply to Christ's coming again and Israel in the future kingdom. Why? Christ was to remain in heaven until the restitution occurred (reread verse 21). Secondly, when it occurs, then everything will be restored to what it was. This restoration is not talking about doctrine, i.e. the gospel and God's truth, which cannot be lost (Psalm 100:5). What it is talking about is earth being restored to the direct rulership of God as it was before Adam and Eve sinned. This restoration also involves Israel being in their land and worshiping the true God (Ezekiel 37:1-14). Israel is in the land today, but they are not worshiping the true God. Therefore the gospel (which has never been lost) will continue to be preached in all nations before His coming to set up the millennial kingdom (Acts 1:8).

Ten

Religion's Failure

This book has been a study in how to reach people of the cults and multiple world religions with the message of Christ, but why should we do so? Why witness to religious people? Christians usually do not question the need to send missionaries to impoverished countries, "darkest Africa", or the religiously uncommitted, but why bother someone who is already religious? The answer rests in understanding the nature of religion. (Incidentally, "darkest Africa" probably has some of the most religious people to be found anywhere in the world!)

First, Christ commands us to obey the Great Commission of sharing the gospel (Matthew 28:18-20). Religion with all of its efforts worldwide does not satisfy the Great Commission. Religion only imitates it. People are not saved through a religious system of works; they are saved through Christ.

Secondly, good people go to hell (Matthew 7:21-23) because religion chooses its way over God's way.

In Psalm 14:2-3, God looked down from heaven on humanity to see if He could discover someone seeking after Him. He states that He found none. That comment is mind-blowing. I look around at the world, and I see millions of people who at least seem to be seeking after God. Why would God say such a thing? The answer is the biblical base for religion's failure. The people of the world, no matter how religious, are not seeking God in God's way. Religion, by its very nature of sinful man needing to work his way to the holy God, is doomed for failure. Religious people fail to understand the issues at stake (Romans 10:3).

This business of salvation is serious. We used Mormon doctrine for many of our examples in this book. Let's talk about them for a moment, respectfully. Millions of Mormons are on our planet today. By their own statistics, every two and a half minutes someone in the world becomes a Mormon. [15] In addition to the Mormons, countless other cults and religions are growing rapidly throughout the world. We cannot ignore them and hope that someday they will go away. The next person becoming a Mormon may very well be your daughter or father or wife or even you. The people of the cults are good people who live moral lives. Yet, the Bible teaches that this goodness is not enough. Everyone must come to the biblical Christ in order to reach God.

The world is filled with many organized belief systems, whether we call them cults or religions, Christian or pagan. The Bible warns that a religion creates barriers that prevent its people from being with God when they die. The barriers are tragic but not always obvious. By way of review, here are some sobering facts about the falseness of religion (the barriers) and why religion is so dangerous.

False Authority

2 Corinthians 2:17 warns that, already in Paul's day, people were trying to corrupt the Word of God. Destroying people's confidence in the Bible is an absolute necessity to control their thinking in a religious system. Cults exist and thrive on authority outside the Bible. Remember their threefold approach:

1. "The Bible has errors, and you need our corrections."
2. "The Bible cannot be understood without our leaders' interpretation."
3. "The Bible is not complete, and you need our additional scriptures."

False authority involves false apostles and teachers (2 Corinthians 11:13-15) and false prophets (Matthew 24:11). In 1 John 4:1 we read, *"Beloved, believe not every spirit, but try the spirits whether they are of God: because many false prophets are gone out into the world."* It would be nice if Satan's workers were required to wear a sign saying: I AM FROM SATAN! That label would make them easy to identify. Finally, false authority ultimately leads to false doctrine and massive error (1 Timothy 4:1).

False Gospel

In a now very familiar passage, Galatians 1:6-9, Paul warns against a perverted gospel message that does not teach the grace of God (v. 6). False news is never good news, no matter how sincere! The wrong gospel leads to a false righteousness (Romans 10:1-3) and false godliness (2 Timothy 3:5, 7). Religion promotes the great heavenly scales concept! If my "good" will simply outweigh my "bad", God will overlook my "bad". People simply do not understand how pure God is. The holy God observes the religious efforts of mankind and labels their actions as filthy rags (Isaiah 64:6).

An illustration I use with children says this truth simply enough. If I took a turkey dinner with all the trimmings and mixed in last week's garbage, would you still want to eat it? No matter how good the turkey is, it is still mixed with garbage. No matter how good a person becomes, he must deal with the sin issue God's way, or God will reject him.

False Jesus

Paul warned about spiritual fakes being titled "Jesus" (2 Corinthians 11:3-4). The claims of a church, organization, or religious group to believe in Jesus do not mean that they believe in the Jesus of the Bible. Jesus Himself warned against false Christs (Matthew 24:5, 23-24). Ultimately, a false Jesus leads to a false way (John 14:6). Just because people are religious and/or believe in God, does not mean they are saved, no two ways about it! Christianity is unique in the religious world. The tragedy is that religious people are working to be with God, when God in reality has done the work to be with people.

Urgency of the Gospel

People desperately want acceptance and seek it where it can be found. Time is running out! Our lifestyle must be to live and share Christ (Acts 18:27). We can no longer dare to take for granted that our religious friends and relatives are saved.

We have a very real responsibility not to accept at face value what anyone says is biblical. We must examine every Jesus presented to us in the light of who the biblical Jesus really is. If the one sharing with us his personal belief has a false Jesus, we are not to hate and ridicule him. We are to present the real Christ in love, even though this lost one rejects our message (Ezekiel 2:3-5). Why? Because if not for the grace of God, we could be as he is.

I remember as a missionary pastor in Utah being called to an emergency at the local hospital. After spending time with the people I had come to visit, I sat for a few minutes in the waiting section of the emergency room. About then, I heard a siren grow in intensity until it screamed loudly at the emergency entrance. I looked up to watch a couple of paramedics wheeling in a man on a stretcher. The whole front of this person's face was missing. His head was covered with blood. After a few minutes, the ambulance driver, who had entered a moment later than the others, came over to get a drink from a water fountain near where I was sitting.

"Does that patient have a chance to make it at all?" I asked.

The driver shook his head and said, "Not at all. He will probably be dead in just a few minutes."

"What happened?"

"A motorcycle wreck," came the reply as the man walked off.

Just a few minutes, and this person would be in eternity. *Was he a Mormon?* I wondered. Probably he was. After all, this hospital was in Utah Valley, and Utah Valley is ninety-five percent Mormon. With minutes until eternity, there was no way to help this man.

Then I heard a scream behind me. I turned to see several ladies and a Mormon bishop escorting a sobbing woman into a prayer room next to where I sat. I was amazed that they didn't close the door. I moved away to respect their privacy, but I could still hear the woman weeping inside the room.

The Mormon bishop was seeking to console her, and I realized from what he was saying that she was the wife of the man from the motorcycle wreck. Apparently, he had just died. The bishop kept repeating to the grief-stricken woman that everything would be all right, because she and her husband had been married in the temple. I will never forget her reply.

She screamed, "It's not enough! It's not enough!"

IT IS NOT ENOUGH.

Appendix

Research Section

1. Witnessing to people in religions and cults is challenging, but not impossible. The same gospel that saved you will save religious people in the cults or otherwise, despite the terminology difficulties. Definitions, however, are important, and learning them will be very helpful! Define the meaning of each of the following biblical and theological terms in simple English.

   Salvation/Saved
   Eternal Life
   Resurrection
   Believe/Trust
   Faith
   Grace
   Sin
   Repentance
   Born Again
   Baptism
   Scripture
   Priesthood

Angel
Trinity
Godhead
Jehovah
Son of God
Child of God

2. Memorize the following references under each topic. Look up each verse and write what it means. Learn the meaning of each reference. Answer any questions listed with the verses. Learning all of the verses isn't necessary, but the more you learn, the more prepared you'll be!

Sin and Rebellion
Isaiah 64:6 (How does God view religious righteousness?)
Romans 3:23
Romans 6:23

Gospel
1 Corinthians 15:1-4 (What is the gospel?)
Galatians 1:6-9 (Can there be another gospel besides grace?)

Christ's Death
Isaiah 53:5-6 (Was Christ a substitute?)
John 3:16
Romans 5:8

Salvation
John 1:12 (What does believing or trusting in Christ mean?)
John 14:6 (How many ways are there to God?)
Acts 16:31
Romans 10:9-10, 13
Galatians 3:26 (How does one become a child of God?)
1 John 5:9-13 (How can we know we have eternal life?)

Grace and Works
Isaiah 55:1 (Can you buy salvation?)
John 6:28-29 (Who does the work in salvation?)
Ephesians 2:8-10 (What relationship exists between works and salvation?)
Romans 11:6 (Can we mix grace and works to be saved?)
Titus 3:5

Baptism
Acts 8:36-37
Acts 10:43 (Is baptism necessary for the forgiveness of sins?)
1 Corinthians 1:17 (Is baptism part of the gospel?)

Eternal Security
John 10:27-29
Romans 8:35-39
Ephesians 1:12-14 (How long is a person sealed by the Holy Spirit?)

Philippians 1:6
Jude 24

God's Judgment
Luke 16:19-31 (Can a person travel back and forth between heaven and hell?)
John 3:18
John 3:36
Hebrews 9:27 (What takes place immediately after death?)

Trinity
Matthew 28:19 (Is "name" singular or plural? Are there three Gods or one?)
John 10:30
Isaiah 48:12, 16 (Who is speaking in verse 12, and who sends Him?)
1 John 5:7

Only One God
Deuteronomy 4:39 (Can other gods exist in the universe?)
Deuteronomy 6:4
Isaiah 43:10
Isaiah 44:6, 8
Isaiah 45:18, 22

Nature of God
Psalm 90:2 (Did God have a beginning?)
Malachi 3:6
John 1:18
John 4:24/Luke 24:39 (Does God have a body?)

Numbers 23:19 (Was God ever a man?)
Hosea 11:9

Jesus Christ
John 1:1, 14 (Who is the Word?)
John 20:28
1 Timothy 3:16

Holy Spirit
John 7:37-39 (When does a person receive the Holy Spirit?)
Acts 5:3-4 (Is the Holy Spirit God?)

Bible Complete
John 16:13 (What is "all truth"?)
2 Timothy 3:15-17
Hebrews 1:1-2 (Do we have prophets or continuous revelation today?)
Revelation 22:18-19

Truth of God Cannot Be Lost
Psalm 100:5
Isaiah 40:8
Isaiah 59:21 (Has God preserved His Word in heaven only?)
1 Peter 1:23 (Can the Bible become corrupt?)
Jude 3 (How many times has God delivered His truth?)

Priesthood
Matthew 27:51 (Why did the veil tear apart?)

Hebrews 7:22-25 (Does Jesus' priesthood change from one person to another?)

No Preexistence
John 3:13 (Is Jesus the only one that has come down from heaven to receive an earthly body?)
1 Corinthians 15:46 (Which is first: the spiritual existence or the physical?)
Romans 9:11 (Could we have done right or wrong in an existence before coming to earth?)

Marriage in Heaven
Matthew 22:23-30 (If we are married on earth, will we be married in heaven?)

3. Some religions and cults often use particular passages in an unscriptural way. Having a proper understanding of these passages is important. Write the biblical meaning to the following references.

James 2:14-26
Matthew 24:13
Philippians 2:12
John 3:5
Acts 2:38
Mark 16:16
Acts 22:16
1 Peter 3:18-21
1 Peter 4:6
1 Corinthians 15:29
Hebrews 6:4-6

Endnotes

1. *Random House Webster's College Dictionary,* 2nd ed., s.v. "Cult."

2. Ezra Taft Benson (devotional, Brigham Young University, Provo, UT, February 22, 1980).

3. "Priesthood News Evokes Joy," *Deseret News,* June 17, 1978.

4. Gary Vertican, personal communication to author, 2000.

5. Bruce R. McConkie, *Mormon Doctrine* (Salt Lake City: Bookcraft, 1966), 169, 240, 256-258, 321, 323, 576, 577.

6. *What the Mormons Think of Christ* (Salt Lake City: Deseret Press, 1973), 31. (The 1982 edition has the statement on p. 19-20. Later editions have removed the statement altogether.)

7. Creative Bible Study, August 15, 2009, http://www.creativebiblestudy.com/Blondin-story.html.

8. Demosthenes *Olynthica* 3.19.

9. Lloyd Larkin, personal communication to author, 1973. (Additional examples and information are available in Mr. Larkin's pamphlets *Ministering to*

Mormons, Latter-day Sense from the Bible, and *Let's Discuss Scripture – Biblical Answers to Mormon Questions,* available through Baptist Mid-Missions, PO Box 308011, Cleveland, OH 44130-8011.)
10. Martin R. Dahlquist (lecture, Spurgeon Baptist Bible College, Mulberry, FL, 1979).
11. Dr. Robert L. Sumner, *Does the Bible Teach That Water Baptism Is a Necessary Requirement for Salvation?* (Raleigh, NC: Biblical Evangelist, 1970).
12. Paul Tassel (sermon, Spurgeon Baptist Bible College, Mulberry, FL, 1979).
13. Lloyd Larkin, personal communication to author, 1985.
14. Chris A. Vlachos, email to author, June 8, 1998.
15. "The Book of Mormon...Can It Add To Your Life?", *Readers Digest,* 1981, 2 of magazine insert.

LaVergne, TN USA
10 October 2010
200259LV00001B/2/P